Southern Shade

A PLANT SELECTION GUIDE

JO KELLUM, ASLA

UNIVERSITY PRESS OF MISSISSIPPI
JACKSON

in memory of my father

who loved flowers

www.upress.state.ms.us

The University Press of Mississippi is a member of
the Association of American University Presses.

Designed by Todd Lape

Page ii: Windflower (*Anemone blanda*)
Page v: Pinxterbloom azalea (*Rhododendron peridymenoides*)

Photographs courtesy of Jo Kellum unless
otherwise noted

First printing 2008
∞
Library of Congress Cataloging-in-Publication Data

Kellum, Jo.
  Southern shade : a plant selection guide / Jo Kellum.
    p. cm.
  Includes index.
  ISBN-13: 978-1-934110-47-8 (cloth : alk. paper)
  ISBN-10: 1-934110-47-7 (cloth : alk. paper)
  ISBN-13: 978-1-934110-48-5 (pbk. : alk. paper)
  ISBN-10: 1-934110-48-5 (pbk. : alk. paper) 1.
Shade-tolerant plants—Selection—Southern States.
2. Gardening in the shade—Southern States. I. Title.
  SB434.7K46 2008
  635.9′5430975—dc22   2007028020

British Library Cataloging-in-Publication Data available

Contents

Bedding Plants

PERENNIALS: BEDDING PLANTS THAT COME BACK

ANNUALS: SINGLE-SEASON BEDDING PLANTS

Shrubs

Trees

Groundcovers

Vines

Acknowledgments

Special thanks to Ray, my best friend who shared his name with me, and to Emma, who is genetically programmed to hum, design, write, and talk to cats.

Thank you to my mother, who understood that sometimes puzzle pieces mix together to make soup.

I am also grateful to many wonderful gardeners, both known and unknown to me personally. Among the many others who shared their gardens with me, I thank Lawrence and Jane Akers, Cay and Anne Ozburn, and Bill and Jo Ann Wilkerson.

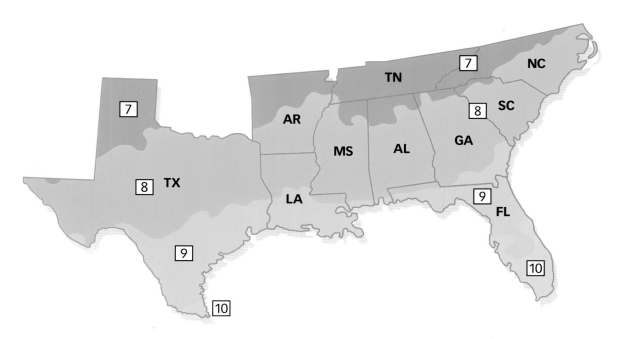

MAP OF SOUTHERN GARDENING ZONES

The upper portion of a zone is the area that is most
northerly. The lower portion is more southerly. This
can be confusing because lower zones have higher
zone numbers; nonetheless, within the following
pages, upper means northerly, in keeping with
horticultural tradition.

Introduction

I always wonder what that little half-black and half-yellow sun shown on plant tags really means. It's not hard to figure out that the plants bearing this designation need some sun and some shade, but how much of each, and when? Shade in the South is a peculiar animal. Spots in your landscape that are deeply shaded in summer may be bright and sunny in winter, and afternoon shade is vastly different from morning shade. Set one of those half-and-half tagged plants in the wrong kind of shade, and you may as well have flipped a coin to decide where to plant it.

This book strives to offer planting advice that's specific to our region. For example, some plants need a dose of sunlight to flower but can't take the blazing rays that slant from the west on summer afternoons in the South. These are plants that require morning sun followed by afternoon shade during the hot months, and they're noted as such in the pages that follow. Seasonal shade needs are also identified per plant. Sometimes the planting instructions included here vary according to where you live. Take a look at the Southern Gardening Zone map, locate your little corner of the world, and note the corresponding zone number. Any plant that includes that zone number within its range is suitable for your area. But read on to find more specific information about particular conditions that may exist in your own garden.

If you're armed with enough information to put the right plant in the right place, landscaping satisfaction is well within reach. As a landscape architect myself, my interest isn't limited to merely helping you keep plants alive. That's why I've included plenty of notes about what different plants can do for you, too. After all, the goal is to put plants where you need them, where they belong, where they'll be easy to maintain, and where you'll enjoy them the most.

The whole idea behind *Southern Shade* is putting the right plant in the right place. Because shade in the South isn't like shade elsewhere, this book strives to address gardening in shade as we know it. If sun is another challenge you face, take a look at *Southern Sun*, the companion book to this one. Though making a dent in the botanical bounty of the South would require multiple volumes of each book, I've selected plants to share with you that come in a range of colors, sizes, shapes, and problem-solving capabilities. Grow happy.

Bedding Plants

Perennials
BEDDING PLANTS THAT COME BACK

Astilbe

Astilbe hybrid

Also sold as false spirea, perennial spirea, meadowsweet, florist's spirea

I t is no surprise that a flower as delectable as astilbe would require the best of soils. Grow it if you're naturally blessed with woodsy soil that's fertile and consistently moist. Or, grow it if you're dedicated enough to do what it takes to keep astilbe happy. Either way, you'll be rewarded for your hospitality with divine summer blossoms that recall a long ago time when ladies wore feathered hats. Each flowery plume of astilbe is branched and coated with thousands of tiny blooms and held above mounded foliage by a wiry stem. When watering is consistently adequate, the show lasts for a month or more. Hybridized astilbes offer an amazing range of flower color choices.

Astilbe needs shade in hot climates. A little sun is necessary for flowering, but make sure plants are protected from direct noonday sun and those blazing western rays late in the day. With a little observation, the shade/sun issue can be figured out pretty quickly. It is the combination of moisture and shade requirements that makes growing astilbe in the South tricky. Shady areas commonly have soil that's quite dry due to water-hogging tree roots. But trees are necessary to create shade. One good way out of this pickle is to grow astilbe in wooded locations where leaves have piled up and decayed in layers for years. Such natural areas are more likely to retain moisture at ground level than gardens that are raked clean each autumn. Another prime location for astilbe is beside a shaded pond or stream. The damp soil at water's edge is ideal.

If neither of these options exists in your own landscape, you can create an astilbe kingdom. It will take some effort to roll out the red carpet, but most of the work is done once. Start by finding a spot that's mostly shaded

GETTING ACQUAINTED

Perennial bedding plant

Sizes vary by selection; average size is 12 to 18 inches high by 18 to 24 inches wide; forms spreading clumps

Plumes of delicately textured flowers are held above foliage in summer; many colors available from white, pink, lavender, red, and yellow to in-between shades such as burgundy

Resistant to insects

Moderate to slow rate of growth

Partial shade; protect from hot afternoon sun

Fertile soil that's evenly moist; not for poor or dry soil

Good choice for woodland gardens, shaded courtyards, pond sides, stream banks, and moist beds of rich soil

Pairs well with Virginia sweetspire, hosta, foamflower, trillium, wishbone flower, bluestar, impatiens, celandine poppy, hydrangeas, Virginia bluebell, red buckeye, Solomon's seal, Japanese maple, Japanese painted fern, caladium, pieris, fothergilla, cardinal flower, Lenten rose, and windflower

Zones 4–9

Delicate, shade-loving astilbe shows off well before a background of coarse oakleaf hydrangea.

A

B

C

but receives some morning sun. Next, mix plenty of humus and peat moss into the soil to make it richly fertile and slightly acidic. Dig at least 1 foot deep and turn over the existing soil so the amendments are spread throughout the bed. Till them in if you can avoid damaging tree roots. Your improved soil should be dark and crumbly but just a little sticky when squeezed—kind of like chocolate cake.

Set young astilbe plants 12 to 18 inches apart within the prepared bed. Be sure to stagger the plants like a checkerboard so they'll fill in faster. After planting, soak the bed gently with water. When the plot is still damp yet has become dry enough to work in, spread a layer of fine compost across the bed's surface, tucking it around each plant while staying several inches away from stems. This is called topdressing. Twine a soaker hose among the plants. Then cover the whole bed, including the hose, with a light layer of pine straw. Pull straw back like a little porthole around each plant.

If you're going to go to all the trouble it takes to invite such horticultural royalty to your garden, you may as well grow a lot of them. Astilbe looks best when multiples of the same plant are grown together as a solid mass. Plant this perennial in single-color drifts; the effect will be breathtaking at blossom time. Astilbe's fluffy foliage is very attractive, too, and it shows up more when you grow a bunch of it together. Leaves are shiny and finely cut and often compared to ferns. Plants spread and live for years.

Once you've gotten astilbe going, you'll need to check soil moisture frequently by poking a finger into the dirt. Water regularly with the soaker hose. For the first two years, you'll need to apply as much as 1 inch of water per week to your astilbe bed during hot seasons. Established plants can get by with slightly less water, but they'll always need consistent moisture to thrive, especially in summer. Feed plants in spring using a 5–10–5 fertilizer per manufacturer's instructions. Afterward, reapply topdressing of fine compost and pine straw mulch to prepare astilbe for another summer of heavenly blooms.

(A) White or cream-colored flowers are always a good choice for shade. They seem to linger in summer twilight.
(B) Pastel colors shine delicately in the shade, but astilbe offers a range of brighter hues, too. This vivid lilac selection is called 'Visions'. *Photo courtesy of the Crownsville Nursery*
(C) The foliage of astilbe dies down in winter, but wait until spring to cut it to help keep plants cold-hardy. Fresh greenery will emerge before the blossoms do.

Dicentra spectabilis

Also sold as common bleeding heart

GETTING ACQUAINTED

Perennial bedding plant

1 to 3 feet tall and wide

Heart-shaped flowers dangle from arched stems from mid to late spring; finely cut foliage

Slow rate of growth

Partial shade to all-day shade; protect from hot afternoon sun

Fertile, moist soil that drains well; established plants tolerate dry conditions in adequate shade; not for alkaline soil or permanently wet soil

Good choice for woodland gardens, tucked into shady perennial beds, rock gardens, niches, and courtyards or grow along the high sides of ponds or the foot of shade-loving shrubs

Pairs well with hosta, bluestar, mondo grass, daffodil, Virginia sweetspire, rhododendron, hydrangeas, foamflower, celandine poppy, Solomon's seal, Japanese painted fern, holly fern, Japanese maple, red buckeye, pieris, Lenten rose, trillium, Virginia bluebell, and ferns

Zones 3–9 (not long-lived in lower zone 8 or zone 9)

If you've got shade and woodsy soil, it would be a crime of passion to omit bleeding heart from your garden.

Bleeding Heart

Bleeding heart is the jewelry of the shade garden. Heart-shaped flowers dangle like living lockets when this old-fashioned perennial is in bloom. The blossoms are suspended in rows from arching stems that curve over mounds of delicate foliage. Grow a little bleeding heart for an understated look. Or, grow a lot for glamour in the shadows.

Bleeding heart thrives in woodland conditions of dappled shade and moist soil made rich by rotting leaves. You can also cultivate this dainty plant in beds that receive morning rays but are shaded in the afternoon. Bleeding heart will grow in all-day shade, too, but it flowers better with a dose of sunlight. Avoid blazing hot locations. The farther south you live, the more shade your bleeding heart will require. Don't plant it close to tree roots, where the topsoil tends to stay dry.

If your soil is so-so—not difficult to turn over with a trowel but not necessarily moist, either—go ahead and give bleeding heart a try. Pick a spot that's shady at midday and throughout the afternoon. Start with one plant and resolve to water it through its first spring. (But beware of overwatering; despite its need for moisture, bleeding heart roots will rot if they're kept too wet.) Dig a hole that's twice as wide as it is deep and mix in a generous helping of compost or decayed leaves when planting. Mulch well to help keep the soil around your bleeding heart cool and moist. Water frequently. By the second spring, your plant will probably be able to thrive on natural rainfall supplemented with an occasional squirt from the hose. If your plant flushes out nicely and produces more growth than the year before, you can claim success. You can also go buy some more bleeding hearts.

Flowering increases with age as plants spread to form denser, wider clumps. When blooming finishes, bleeding heart persists as a pretty bed of

fine foliage. For a while, that is. By midsummer, leaves yellow and wither. This is perfectly normal; there's no need to panic. Bleeding heart goes dormant in hot weather. Resist the urge to water heavily. Doing so won't bring the foliage back but it may cause roots to rot. Let the foliage die completely to the ground before cutting it off. If the appearance isn't bothering you, leave the dead leaves and stems alone and they'll fade away completely. Because there's no need to water withering foliage or dormant roots, the major watering effort to get bleeding heart established is limited to spring. That makes the prospect of adding this perennial to your garden a lot more appealing. If you can find it for sale, you can also start bleeding heart in autumn for blooms the following spring. Keep autumn-planted bleeding hearts moist, but cut back on watering when temperatures drop. Stop altogether when leaves begin to yellow.

Plant bleeding heart where you can enjoy the delicate blossoms up close. It is lovely growing beside benches and pathways, at entry areas, and tucked into the fronts of beds at the foot of shrubs or summer perennials. Hosta, astilbe, and ferns are good companions to mingle with bleeding heart. Their foliage will help hide bleeding heart's absence in summer and autumn.

(A) Dainty bleeding heart makes a fluffy mound in spring.
(B) White-flowering bleeding heart pairs well with the regular pink-flowering plant.
(C) Don't fret when bleeding heart leaves turn yellow and wither away in summer. This plant's dormancy is triggered by heat; there's no need to water.
(D) This delicate perennial blooms the same time as many daffodil selections.

BLEEDING HEART

NAMED SELECTIONS

If a bleeding heart has no name on it other than *Dicentra spectabilis*, it is a species plant, and you can assume that the flowers will be pink with white centers. The named selections listed below have been cultivated to emphasize certain characteristics.

'GOLDHEART': showy lime green foliage, larger leaves; bright pink flowers; may be a little trickier to get established

'ALBA': white flowers

'CANDY HEARTS': solid pink flowers (no white centers); blooms longer than the species plant

'IVORY HEARTS': solid white flowers; blooms longer than species plant

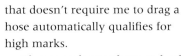

Amsonia tabernaemontana

Also sold as willow bluestar, amsonia, bluestar flower, blue dogbane, common bluestar, eastern bluestar

GETTING ACQUAINTED

Perennial bedding plant

3 to 4 feet high and wide

Pale blue flowers open in starry clusters in midspring

Slow rate of growth

Tolerant of drought and cold

Resistant to insects and diseases

Native

Partial shade to full sun; watering needs increase and blossom color fades in full sun

Any soil, wet to dry, fertile to poor

Good choice for perennial beds, woodsy gardens, pond side, creek banks, natural areas, cottage gardens, boggy areas, roadsides, butterfly gardens, and coastal landscapes

Pairs well with dogwood, daffodil, Japanese kerria, foamflower, Virginia sweetspire, aucuba, rhododendron, mondo grass, camellia, yellow archangel, cardinal flower, dead nettle, holly fern, celandine poppy, fothergilla, Pinxterbloom azalea, Lenten rose, oakleaf hydrangea, Spanish bluebell, astilbe, bleeding heart, gooseneck loosestrife, hosta, Solomon's seal, trillium, caladium, impatiens, melampodium, leatherleaf mahonia, periwinkle, smilax, and star magnolia

Zones 3–9

Adaptability is one of bluestar's finest qualities. This native perennial grows in wet or dry soil, partial shade or sun, and it doesn't mind heat or cold.

Bluestar

Bluestar is a master of deception. Its rounded clusters of sky-blue flowers are dainty enough to make this perennial look like it requires an expert's touch to grow. But in truth, bluestar is close to foolproof. It is native to the eastern United States, so you can call it a wildflower while letting it grow unaided like a weed. Bluestar will thrive in just about any soil. This plant's tolerance of wet feet means you can grow it beside ponds and creeks. In dry to average soil, mulch set around the roots of established bluestars helps preserve moisture, and you'll rarely have to supplement natural rainfall. I don't know about you, but a plant

that doesn't require me to drag a hose automatically qualifies for high marks.

Bluestar tolerates heat and cold and comes back reliably from roots year after year. Clumps enlarge slowly, a trait that keeps this native plant from spreading uncontrollably. When grown in partial shade, bluestar stays around 3 feet in height. All-day shade can make plants tall and leggy. Stalks reaching for sunlight become long and weak and may flop over under the weight of flowers, so it is best to grow bluestar where it can receive some sun. Dappled sunlight throughout the day is fine and so is a half-day's worth of sun. Bluestar can take morning or afternoon sun; there's no need to protect it from hot afternoon rays. Bluestar is a particularly useful plant for partially shaded spots where other tall, flowering perennials concede to blossom only with reduced vigor. A bluestar in bloom attracts butterflies to the shade.

The five-pointed flowers, clustered like bouquets, appear in mid to late spring. Tall, branching stalks covered with light green leaves first fill out to form a bushy clump. Flowering lasts for a few weeks. After that, narrow willowy leaves keep bluestar attractive through summer and

A

B

autumn. Long pods resembling pencils are filled with odd log-shaped seeds that can be tricky to germinate. Seeds dropped naturally when pods split in autumn may sprout the following spring and enlarge plant clumps. Foliage turns yellow in late autumn following a hard freeze. After leaves drop, cut all the stalks back to the ground for the winter. New growth will emerge in spring. In early summer, you can trim stalks back a little after flowering finishes, giving plants a light haircut to keep them dense and bushy. Or, you can leave bluestar alone until winter and revel in its easy durability.

(A) Grow bluestar in spots where its winter absence won't be noticeable. Nearby evergreen shrubs will help prevent beds from going empty during the cold months.
(B) It is easy to remember bluestar's name once you've seen it in bloom.

BLUESTAR

NAMED SELECTION

'Blue Ice' is a cultivar that grows wider than it does tall. Each clump spreads to 2 feet across, but the stalks are not much more than a foot high. Flowers may be deeper blue and last longer than the species plant.

Lobelia cardinalis

Also sold as red lobelia

GETTING ACQUAINTED

Perennial bedding plant

3 to 4 feet high by 1 foot wide; occasionally 6
    feet high

Brilliant red spikes of flowers in late summer
    and autumn

Slow rate of growth

Short-lived but reseeds readily in moist, fertile
    soil

Partial shade; protect from afternoon sun in
    hot climates

Moist to wet soil; will grow in shallow standing
    water; not for dry soil

Good choice for boggy areas, wet soil, ponds,
    streams, damp ditches, wildflower gardens,
    and hummingbird and butterfly gardens

Pairs well with Virginia sweetspire, bluestar,
    hydrangeas, fothergilla, and astilbe. Grows
    well in the sun with elephant ear (*Colocasia
    esculenta*)

Zones 4–10

Cardinal flower spikes bloom from the bottom up.
Because stems continue to lengthen and produce
more buds at the top, a single cardinal flower can
bloom for months.

Cardinal Flower

I f you have soil that's wet, don't fret. Cardinal flower loves the soggy
stuff. This striking wildflower thrives in damp places and will even
grow in shallow standing water. It dislikes dry soil, so if you have
a spot that's moist enough to grow it, consider yourself lucky. Ponds,
streams, marshes, boggy areas, and over-irrigated spots are prime cardinal
flower territory.

Cardinal flowers are inconspicuous additions to the garden—at first.
Small rosettes of foliage squat at ground level through the winter and into
spring. A central stem sprouts and grows 2 to 4 feet tall by late summer.
Purplish leaves surround the stem. Then the fun begins. The stem goes
into high gear, putting on another 1 or 2 feet of growth quite quickly.

Foliage grown here is mostly green.
Vivid red flowers begin to open
along the topmost 8 to 12 inches;
some plants produce flower spikes
that are 2 feet in length. The tip of
the plant's stem continues to elongate and the flowers keep opening.
Blooming may last into October.
The multiple blossoms serve as bea-
cons for ruby-throated hummingbirds, which pollinate the plants.
The hummers can't resist the call
so you'll get to enjoy both flowers
and flyers. The flowering period
coincides neatly with hummingbird
migration schedules, enabling cardinal flowers to function as service
stations for these tiny birds during
their travels.

Though cardinal flowers are
native to marshy spots across much
of the country, they're unfortunately absent from many retail
nurseries. Stores or online nurseries specializing in water gardening,
wildflowers, or other native species may be the best sources. You can start
with plants or seeds. Cardinal flower blooms during its second year, so

A

B

you'll have to wait a while for flowers if you sow seeds. Plants purchased in nursery pots are more likely to bloom during their first summer in your garden, especially if you get them in the ground the previous autumn. If cardinal flowers are planted in early spring, you may or may not enjoy blooms that August. Plants that don't bloom the first year will flower the second.

Cardinal flowers are short-lived, so it is important to keep new generations underway to replenish your garden. Each bloom spike produces thousands of seeds, giving you ample opportunity to provide nature with a little assistance. Seedpods ripen from the bottom of the bloom first and follow an upward order along the spent flower spike. In late autumn when pods are dry, wrinkled, and brown, bend each stalk over so you can insert the top portion into a bag and shake it well. Pods must be ripe enough to split to release their bounty of seeds. You can start this process as soon as the lower pods ripen. Repeat it a few times intermittently for about a month to harvest seeds from pods higher on the same stalk. You should wind up with a lot more of the tiny, dustlike seeds than you need, but don't worry, they won't all sprout.

In November, scatter seeds across the surface of wet or damp soil, including mossy spots. Cardinal flowers need sunlight to germinate, so don't cover seeds with soil or even scratch them into the surface. Because

(A) Hummingbirds and butterflies are quite fond of the nectar of this startlingly red flower.
(B) Cardinal flower is native, so you may find it growing wild in damp roadside ditches. It is suitable for growing in formal water gardens as well.

a layer of fallen leaves can block the sun's rays and prevent germination, it's a good idea to keep your seeded patches tidy. Seeds sprout in spring. The first rosettes of foliage are quite small, so don't step on them or rake them away by mistake. Plants grow slowly during their freshman year, remaining squatty through the first winter. Do not mulch them else roots may rot. Stalks appear the second summer, yielding those amazing redder-than-red flowers.

Cardinal flowers bloom in full sun in cool regions, but partial shade is advisable in the South. Plants will thrive in all-day dappled shade or situations where they're shaded for half a day. It doesn't matter which half. Cardinal flowers will even bloom in full shade, where the startling red color is particularly welcome, but you won't get as many flowers as you would on plants that receive some sun.

NAMED SELECTIONS

Though the bright red flowers of native cardinal flowers are hard to beat, hybridists have come up with some good cultivars.

'ALBA': white

'ANGEL'S SONG': salmon marked with cream

Monet's Moment®: rosy red spikes up to 3 feet long

'QUEEN VICTORIA': red flowers and reddish leaves

'TWILIGHT ZONE': pink

'RUSSIAN PRINCE': red flowers and purple leaves

KEEP THE FLOWERS COMING

If you've only got a few cardinal flowers, let all the spent flowers fade on their stalks so you'll have plenty of seed to harvest. But if your patch of plants is established, keep some stalks standing for seed production but cut others after flowers fade. By removing the blossom before it forms seeds, you may be able to trick the plant into flowering again. Cut the central stalk at ground level when the topmost blossoms decline. Secondary side shoots may appear and produce another set of blooms.

WATERBORNE

Aquarium aficionados claim their own method of propagating cardinal flowers, which they grow in fish tanks. Some aquascapists recommend floating a cut flower with some stalk attached in a good-sized container of tepid water indoors near a window. The flowers will die but young sprouts with rounded leaves will appear at the base of the buds. These can be separated and planted to grow more cardinal flowers. Such plantlets are likely to require a year in the ground before they'll flower.

Celandine Poppy

Stylophorum diphyllum

Also sold as woody poppy, yellow wood poppy, golden-flowered woodpoppy

Celandine poppy is perfect for shady, damp bare spots beneath trees where fallen leaves collect and grass won't grow. This wildflower grows untended in similar situations in the woods. Plants appear in spring, putting forth low mounds of scalloped, blue-green foliage. Fuzzy buds follow. By midspring, rich yellow flowers open. Each bright bloom is 1 to 2 inches across and resembles a buttercup. When conditions are to their liking, celandine poppies spread to form low-growing colonies. The scattering of cheery yellow blooms across a forest floor or shaded bed is quite eye-catching. The flowers are like dabs of sunshine lighting the shadows.

Evaluate your own landscape for celandine poppy acceptability. Locations that stay moist throughout the warm season are ideal; spots that are wet or damp only in spring will do. These golden-petaled wildflowers prefer areas that are shaded in summer. Because plants need some sunlight in early spring to bloom, celandine poppy is well suited for growing beneath trees that are bare in winter and leafy in summer. The soil in your new poppy bed should be rich in organic matter. If your soil seems dry and pale, mix in generous amounts of compost. You can add nursery-grown plants in spring or autumn. Set young plants level with adjacent soil. After planting, soak roots with a trickling hose and surround them with mulch to retain moisture.

Or, start a celandine poppy patch from seed after the last frost. If your soil is fertile from layers of rotted leaves, you won't need to go to much effort. First, rake away dry, dead leaves to expose rich, moist topsoil—there's no need to remove chunks of decaying matter. Next, scatter the seeds generously by hand as if you were planting grass. Don't cover the

GETTING ACQUAINTED

Perennial bedding plant

10 to 18 inches high and wide

Yellow flowers on short stems cover plants in spring; often mistaken for buttercups

Rapid rate of growth

May be invasive given ideal conditions

Resistant to insects and disease

Partial shade to all-day shade; blooms best with some sun in late winter and early spring; protect from summer sun

Rich, woodsy soil that's moist in spring; okay if soil is dry in summer; not for compacted soil

Good choice for woodland gardens, beds that are shady and moist, wildflower gardens, natural areas, and growing along paths

Pairs well with Virginia bluebell, bleeding heart, astilbe, hosta, foamflower, bluestar, fothergilla, Solomon's seal, Japanese maple, trillium, star magnolia, Japanese painted fern, Lenten rose, red buckeye, windflower, mondo grass, and hydrangeas

Zones 4–9

You may want to grow celandine poppies mixed with shade-loving plants that have summer foliage. This makes the poppies' summer absence less noticeable. Hosta, mondo grass, astilbe, ferns, and summer annuals can do the trick.

A

B

seeds. Spray the seeded bed gently with just enough water to moisten the surface and then leave it alone. Celandine poppy seeds don't keep well, so the rate of germination is improved if you start with fresh seeds. To collect seeds from existing plants, watch for the development of fuzzy green seed-pods in flower centers after petals drop. When pods turn tan and begin developing vertical cracks, it is time to collect the tiny black seeds by shaking them into a bag. Pods ripen and release their contents quickly, so pay attention to plants to keep from missing out on the bounty. Sow harvested seeds as soon as possible. Check local ordinances before collecting seeds from the wild; celandine poppies may be a protected native species in your area.

If you've already gotten a few plants established, you can let them drop seeds on their own to thicken the existing poppy patch. Don't be alarmed if you notice ants in the bed. These tiny insects are natural planters of celandine poppy seeds. An outer segment of the seed, nicknamed ant bread, is eaten by ants. They'll drag seeds one by one to shallow burrows, eat the ant bread, and leave the remaining seeds intact underground, where they can sprout.

Hot, dry conditions force celandine poppies into dormancy, so they disappear from most beds in the South by midsummer. Don't cut withering foliage. Instead, let it fade away on its own. Given regular water, plants will keep leaves until frost and may produce blooms sporadically. But for most gardeners in our climate, it is easiest to simply forget about celandine poppies until they reappear the following spring.

(A) Celandine poppies' bright yellow blooms in the shade are an easy springtime treat.
(B) Virginia bluebells have similar growing requirements and bloom at the same time as celandine poppies. Grow these perennials together for a lovely combination of blue and yellow blossoms that will repeat effortlessly each spring.

Daffodil

Narcissus species

Also sold as jonquil, narcissus

Nothing could be more rewarding than growing daffodils. You stick a few bulbs in the ground in late autumn and cheery flowers arrive the following spring—and the next, and the next, and so on for years and years. Bulbs multiply underground, thickening clumps and widening the daffodil's domain, a process known as naturalizing. You don't have to water daffodils, fertilizing is optional, and any soil will do as long as it is not normally damp. In fact, you really don't have to do much of anything with daffodils beyond planting and enjoying them.

Dividing dense clumps every five or six years is advisable as giving bulbs more elbow room yields more blossoms. Dividing also lets you start free bulbs in other parts of your garden (unless you're generous enough to share your unearthed treasures). Although dividing is recommended for optimal blooms, daffodils can live and flower untended for many years. That's why you may spot them peaking up from a blanket of gray, leafless kudzu in spring where a house once stood. Though their planters are long gone, the daffodils soldier on.

Daffodils bloom best with at least a half-day's sun and they need to receive that for six to eight weeks prior to blooming. Six hours of sunlight per day is best. So why are they included in a book about shade plants? Because in the South, we can count on enough winter sunlight to bring our bulbs into bloom if they're planted beneath branches that are bare when it is cold. Many homeowners delineate sunny and shady areas of their gardens based on summertime evaluations. Using this method, daffodils can be grown in spots that qualify as well shaded. The exception, of course, is shade created by plants that stay green year-round. Evergreen trees such as eastern hemlocks, Leyland cypress, red cedars, Southern

GETTING ACQUAINTED

Perennial bedding plant

Sizes range from 4 to 24 inches high and wide

Spring brings fragrant flowers in shades of yellow and cream with optional trimmings of red, orange, or pink; many sizes, flower forms, and color combinations available

Rapid rate of growth

Resistant to insects, disease, and rodents

Partial shade to all-day sun; needs at least half-day's sun for six to eight weeks from winter to early spring

Any soil that's not wet

Good choice for underplanting in groundcover beds, mixing with other bulbs, perennials, low shrubs, or growing in spots where you'll later plant shallow-rooted annuals; easily grown beneath deciduous trees and in the woods; good for every garden style from formal to natural; grow in containers, beds, planters. Grow them everywhere.

Pairs well with everything except water-loving plants (such as cardinal flower)

Zones 2–8

Daffodil bulbs don't need to be refrigerated the way some tulip bulbs do, but a bit of winter cold is required to bring them into bloom. They're good choices for gardeners across the South, except in frost-free areas.

PAPERWHITES

Paperwhite narcissus, (*Narcissus tazetta papyraceous*) Photo courtesy of Raymond L. Kellum Sr.

The amazingly fragrant white blossoms of paperwhite narcissus grow several to a stalk. Gardeners in rare-frost regions, such as coastal areas, can grow paperwhites in their landscapes. In areas north of lower zone 8, paperwhites may not come back. But anyone can grow them indoors in pots set in sunny windows. Potted paperwhites make great gifts. Their progress is a pleasant reminder that spring is on its way, and the sweet perfume when flowers open indoors is delightful.

DAFFODIL CARE

FADING FOLIAGE

For all their attributes, daffodils do have one downside: The yellow, withered foliage is unappealing. But foliage should not be removed until after it has completely faded and is lying flat on the ground. Even when leaves are tan, if they're upright, they're still producing food for the bulb, so leave them alone. The same goes for green leaves that are flattened by rain or wind. If the foliage doesn't come off easily in your hand, then don't pull it and don't cut it. The bulb is still dependent on foliage that's firmly attached. Combine daffodil bulbs with plants that are fluffy later in the season so fading foliage is less noticeable.

DIVIDING CROWDED CLUMPS

To divide overgrown daffodil clumps with declining flower counts, mark plant locations with golf tees in the spring so you can find them in the autumn after foliage has withered away. Dig slowly to avoid slicing through bulbs. Lift entire clumps and gently separate bulblets from parent bulbs. If you have to force bulbs apart, they're not ready to be separated.

POTTED DAFFODILS

You can grow daffodils in pots if you get started in autumn. Set bulbs in containers covered with 4 to 5 inches of soil and make sure rainwater can drain through. Move pots to sunny locations in spring for maximum flowering.

PICKING A SITE

Daffodils face the sun. If plants receive sunlight mainly in the morning, the blooms will face east. Flowers will face west if sun slants to their location primarily in the afternoon. Only bulbs grown in all-day sun, including noontime sun, will not face a particularly noticeable direction. You'll want to keep these facts in mind when selecting a site for planting daffodils so you don't end up with all your flowers turning their backs to you.

magnolias, and white pines cast shade throughout the seasons—that's not the kind of shade in which you want to plant daffodil bulbs. Choose a spot that's either in sun year-round or is sunny in winter and much of the spring. Shade in summer and autumn is not a problem for daffodils because bulbs are dormant then. Unlike many shade-loving plants, daffodils do not need to be protected from hot afternoon sun any time of the year.

Daffodils are officially divided into twelve categories as specified by the Royal Horticultural Society of England. But most homeowners don't care about making the distinction between a trumpet, a poeticus, or a wild form. All you've really got to know is what you like. There are daffodils that produce big, classic yellow flowers, teeny-tiny white ones clustered in puffballs, double-flowering types, daffodils with orange eyes, frilly petals, and pink cups. There are tall ones and short ones, early boomers, middle bloomers, and late bloomers. There are more kinds of daffodils than you can shake a stick at, but they're all pretty, they all smell good, and they all come back year after year. You really can't go wrong with any daffodil. They're gorgeous planted in masses of the same named selection together. Daffodils are also one of the few garden plants that look great when a bunch of different cultivars are mixed together. So browse through pictures and descriptions and buy whatever appeals to you. If you live in a coastal or rare-frost area, chat with other gardeners to see which selections they're growing. This will help you choose daffodils that will come back reliably where winters are brief and mild.

It is important to remember that the time to get daffodil fever is in the autumn, not the spring. By the time you see them blooming, it is too late to purchase and plant bulbs for that season. You'll need to give daffodil bulbs a chance to anchor themselves in place with root growth as well as some time spent chilled underground. This means planting ahead.

In the South, we can generally plant daffodils from Thanksgiving to Christmas. If the top layer of soil freezes in your area, you'll need to get bulbs in the ground before then. But you've got to wait until temperatures are starting to drop so your bulbs will remain dormant instead of sprouting too early. If autumn turns out to be a prolonged version of a summer that's hot and wet, newly planted bulbs may rot. So order daffodils early if you're getting your bulbs from northerly locations that may sell out, but store bulbs in a cool, dry place until night temperatures drop. That's the time to plant daffodil bulbs. Come spring, you'll be glad you did.

A

B

C

D

E

F

G

(A) In general, narrow, rounded leaves and small blossoms mean that daffodils are more heat tolerant than large-flowering types with wide, flat foliage. Small-flowering daffodils are also more likely to form large, spreading colonies by naturalizing.

(B) Daffodils come in a multitude of colors and blossom forms. White-flowering types seem to be particularly fragrant.

(C) Early-blooming selections of daffodils herald the coming spring, but they can also get zapped by late freezes. Plants won't be harmed, even by snow and ice, but blossoms will be killed. So if a freeze is predicted, go ahead and pick all the open flowers and stems bearing large, fat buds. Bring them inside and set them in water. You'll get to enjoy springtime blossoms in your home while winter makes its last stand in your garden.

(D) Most daffodils, like this pink-eyed cultivar, are sterile selections, so removing spent flowers won't promote new blossoms—the blooms weren't going to set seed anyway.

(E) Chipmunks and squirrels will feast on crocus and tulip bulbs if they get the chance, cheating gardeners out of expected spring flowers that never appear. But rodents sense that daffodil bulbs are poisonous to them, so they leave *Narcissus* bulbs alone. That's how daffodils like this one continue blooming each spring, long after anyone is around who can remember its name.

(F) The same spot that's quite shady in summer when trees are in their prime can be sunny enough for growing daffodils when branches are bare.

(G) Sturdy stems, longevity, cheerful colors, and pleasant fragrances make daffodils a cut-flower favorite. Trim stems under running water with sharp scissors or pruners and change water in vases frequently to make picked flowers last even longer.

How much effort you want to expend in planting daffodils is probably directly proportional to the amount of money you spend on bulbs. Daffodils can grow from a shallow hole with native soil brushed back into place. Just make sure the bulb sits pointy end up in the hole and has 2 or 3 inches of soil covering the tip. Use this quick dig-and-drop method if you're planting large quantities of bulbs, if you bought discount bulbs left in the bottom of the bin that look a bit shriveled, if you're in a hurry, or if you're just plain lazy. Daffodils are quite forgiving, and chances are you'll have flowers for the picking next spring.

Devoted gardeners who have spent time deliberating among named selections or who have spent more money than they care to admit on bulbs may want to invest a little more effort in planting. To give bulbs the optimum setting, dig holes 8 inches deep and about 1 foot wide. Fill the hole about halfway with a mixture that's one part native soil, one part sand, and one part compost. Add two or three bulbs of the same species set a few inches apart, pointy ends up, and cover with soil mixture so there are 2 or 3 inches over the bulb tips. Water newly planted bulbs once and leave them alone. There's no need to add fertilizer to quality bulbs at planting. Daffodil devotees may feed bulbs each spring with bone meal or a commercial bulb booster product to promote vigorous growth. Daffodils want plenty of water while they're actively growing and blooming, but springtime rains generally fill this need.

Foamflower

Tiarella wherryi

Also sold as Wherry's foamflower,
Tiarella cordifolia var. *collina*, *Tiarella collina*

Here's a little spring wildflower that stays green year-round in most Southern gardens. Foamflower grows neat, low mounds of maple-leaf-shaped foliage. By midspring, creamy blossoms decorate hairy-stemmed spikes held above the leaves. The delicately fluffy flowers are the foam referred to by the plant's name. The contrast between the coarse leaves and the fine-textured flowers is quite showy. Some blooms are blushed with the palest of pinks.

Foamflower pairs well with a multitude of plants that desire the same fertile, moist soil. Unlike the groundcover form of foamflower, *Tiarella cordifolia*, which spreads by runners, this plant stays put nicely. *Tiarella wherryi* is sometimes referred to as clumping foamflower or Wherry's foamflower to distinguish it from the spreading form. You can tuck this plant here and there to fill in empty spots, or use it as an edger plant as the lowest layer in the front of a bed.

Grow foamflower in all-day dark shade or all-day dappled shade. You can also plant it where it receives some sun in the morning, as long as it's sheltered from the bright sun of midday and afternoon during warm seasons. Winter sunlight streaming through bare branches is too weak to damage foliage, so it's not a problem. Foamflower is a cold-hardy native that won't be damaged by freezing temperatures, but foliage may brown and wither during harsh winters in upper zone 8 and zone 7. If that happens, wait until spring to cut back dead foliage. New growth will appear shortly thereafter. Most Southern gardeners can rely on foamflower to have a year-round presence. Tidy patches of greenery may turn an attractive bronze or maroon color after frost.

GETTING ACQUAINTED

Evergreen perennial bedding plant

10 to 12 inches high and wide

Foamy flower spikes appear from early to mid-spring; foliage is evergreen

Moderate rate of growth

Resistant to insects and disease

Native

All-day shade to partial shade; protect from hot afternoon sun

Rich, moist soil that's not wet; not for poor or dry soil

Good choice for moist, shady beds, wildflower gardens, rock gardens, woodland gardens, entries, narrow spaces, courtyards, and for tucking at the foot of taller plants; also useful for edging shaded beds

Pairs well with Lenten rose, Virginia bluebell, astilbe, hosta, bleeding heart, trillium, bluestar, Japanese maple, mondo grass, daffodil, Solomon's Seal, hydrangeas, pieris, Pinxterbloom azalea, rhododendron, red buckeye, fothergilla, celandine poppy, Virginia sweetspire, star magnolia, Japanese painted fern and other ferns

Zones 4–9

Foamflower and Lenten roses pair beautifully and usually bloom together.

A

B

(A) Clumping foamflower, sometimes called Wherry's foamflower, is perfect for tucking into damp, shady nooks.

(B) Foamflower and celandine poppy bloom at the same time and thrive in the same conditions, making them natural partners. Foamflower's leaves help camouflage the poppies' absence during summer dormancy.

RUNNING FOAMFLOWER

There's another foamflower that sends out runners the way a strawberry plant does. It is similar in appearance to Wherry's foamflower and makes a nice groundcover for shady, moist beds. Known as heartleaf foamflower or Allegheny foamflower, this spreading plant is a separate species, *Tiarella cordifolia*. Grow it in the same conditions you would Wherry's foamflower, but be aware that the running type is not quite as heat tolerant as the clump-forming plants. A few of the named selections for running foamflowers include 'Running Tapestry', 'Slickrock', and 'Elizabeth Oliver'.

Foamflower is a little picky about soil. Because it grows wild in the woods, this perennial wants fertile soil that contains plenty of organic matter. Amend beds or planting holes with generous amounts of compost or rotting leaves prior to planting. Both of these amendments are also good choices for mulching the surface of the soil around plants; reapply mulch each spring. You can start with container-grown plants at any time during the warm months or sow seeds in early spring. Water frequently throughout the plant's first year in your garden. Foamflower's drought tolerance increases with age. When grown in adequate shade and rich soil, established plants rarely require supplemental watering except during extreme heat or long periods without rainfall. (Avoid poor, dry soil and hot sun, as plants grown in the wrong conditions will require constant water.)

Foamflower actually prefers dry roots in winter. Soil that's wet or damp during the cold months is not good for this perennial. To avoid root damage, stop watering foamflower after the first frost. If your soil is naturally wet in winter, consider growing foamflower on a slope or in a raised bed or container. Plants grown in such settings are likely to need extra water in summer. The selection 'Oakleaf' has large, lobed leaves and pinkish blooms.

Gooseneck Loosestrife

Lysimachia clethroides

A strong dose of inhospitality may be your best bet for controlling this plant. Gooseneck loosestrife loves moist soil and sun, so grow it in dry soil in the shade. Not that gooseneck loosestrife isn't charming, but be certain you want this visitor to stay forever before extending an invitation.

There's plenty to like about a self-sufficient plant that grows enthusiastically without the least need for assistance. The flowers are lovely and alluring. Tapered, curving spikes are covered with hundreds of tiny white blossoms in summer. The snowy flowerheads all turn to face the same way, like a gaggle of geese looking for a handout. The unusual shaped blooms of gooseneck loosestrife are pretty in the garden and stunning in floral arrangements. Butterflies love the nectar.

But when the life of the party won't go home after the party's over, things can become a little tiresome. Once established, gooseneck loosestrife grows so vigorously that stopping its spread is the only real chore associated with this plant. You won't need to fertilize, water, spray, or prune. Just stick a few plants in the ground and you'll have a flock of flowers in short order. It really is that easy. And that's potentially problematic. Despite its sweet flowers, some gardeners have described the Goosey One's relentless growth in quite unflattering terms.

Though spent flowers set seed, cutting them off won't stop gooseneck loosestrife's spread. This perennial gobbles up garden space by sending roots running underground. New plants pop up from the root growth, endlessly expanding the gooseneck's domain. The way I see it, you have four choices. One, don't grow this plant. You'll miss out on refreshing white flowers during the heat of summer and lush beds of standing-

GETTING ACQUAINTED

Perennial bedding plant

3 feet high and wide; forms spreading beds by root runners

Distinctively shaped white flowers bloom for four to six weeks in summer

Rapid rate of growth

May be invasive given ideal conditions

Partial shade; tolerates afternoon sun

Plant in dry soil to control growth; spreads rapidly in rich, moist soil; tolerant of clay

Good choice for bare areas where nothing else will grow, big open spaces that need to be filled, empty spots beneath shallow-rooted trees such as maples, or gardens where owners are willing to work to keep this plant in check; not for refined gardens with limited space

Pairs well with bluestar, Japanese kerria, liriope, fothergilla, leatherleaf mahonia, Spanish bluebell, eastern hemlock, and yellow archangel

Zones 3–8

Lovely gooseneck loosestrife's main vice is that it is too easy to grow. Give it an inch and it will take the bed . . . or the yard.

21

A

B

room-only foliage, but it you don't have the space or temperament for an aggressive grower, this choice is right for you.

Option number two: Commit to pulling up unwanted goslings by the roots. This is easier done in some gardens than others. Soft, moist soil enables plants to spread more quickly but also yields roots more easily than hard clay soil does. A measure of control by hand-pulling is possible. Some dedicated souls include gooseneck loosestrife in beds designed to attract butterflies. The nodding white flowers are elegant when combined with purple coneflowers in the sun or clumps of bluestar in the shade. But diligence is required to keep the loosestrife from crowding out the other plants over the years.

Door number three: Plant gooseneck loosestrife where nothing but weeds were going to grow anyway. This perennial is attractive and the ability to colonize territory that's alien to most garden flowers is not without merit. You can grow gooseneck loosestrife to fill in a hopelessly barren alley, empty side yard, former driveway, or a gap in the landscape that's beyond the reach of a hose. There's something to be said for giving weeds a run for their money, and starting gooseneck loosestrife intentionally does yield a more cultivated look than a conflagration of mixed weeds.

Finally, you may choose to simply give gooseneck loosestrife plenty of space in which to spread. Once planted, gooseneck loosestrife is here to stay and here to spread, but if there's space for the taking, the harm may be negligible and the benefits noticeable.

Gooseneck loosestrife will bloom in partially shaded areas. All-day dappled shade is fine, as is half-day's shade. This tough plant will grow in full sun, so you don't have to worry about sheltering it from hot afternoon rays except when it is newly transplanted. Deep, all-day shade reduces flowering significantly. Many plants disdain heavy clay soil, but gooseneck loosestrife tackles it gamely. Moist, soft soil that's fertile promotes the fastest growth and widest spread.

(A) After flowering, a thick stand of gooseneck loosestrife is neither noticeable nor offensive. Green summer foliage gives way to a smattering of red and yellow before fading to brown stalks.
(B) The unusual white blooms of gooseneck loosestrife are quite valuable for brightening the shadows of partially shaded beds.

Holly Fern

Cyrtomium falcatum

Also sold as Japanese holly fern, *Cyrtomium falcatum* 'Rochfordianum'

Dense, dark shade is a challenging condition. Though partial shade is agreeable to many plants, the majority of these fizzle when they're planted where the sun never shines. Fortunately, there's holly fern. This shiny-leaved plant thrives in low-light and nearly no-light situations. What's more, holly fern prefers dry feet, so it will grow in that nearly impossible combination of dry shade. Though it is occasionally browned by a cold winter, holly fern is normally evergreen in zones 8 and 9, so you won't have bare spots in your garden in winter.

Holly fern grows in clumps that thicken and widen as plants age. Like any fern, the fronds of holly fern sport multiple leaflets. But instead of fine and feathery foliage, holly fern is known for its big, bold leaflets that resemble holly. The large size of the leaves gives holly fern a coarse texture, making it especially attractive when planted in large groups. You can fill an entire shadowy bed with holly fern and it will look great.

The coarse texture of holly fern also makes an attractive contrast when grown with other plants that have more delicate foliage. Mondo grass, Japanese maple, and other ferns are good fine-textured, shade-loving companions. Holly fern also shows off well beside pathways and patios with patterned surfaces, such as brick, stone, or pea gravel.

Holly fern has three enemies: hot sun, poor drainage, and overwatering. Shade is essential, as strong sun will scorch the leaves. You can plant holly fern in the dark shadows of all-day shade or in areas where the sunlight is filtered throughout the day by overhead tree canopies. These plants can tolerate a little morning sun, but hours of hot rays will cause them to decline.

Holly fern thrives in soil that is rich in organic matter, such as decayed leaves, so add plenty to beds prior to planting. Good drainage is a require-

GETTING ACQUAINTED

Evergreen bedding plant

18 to 24 inches high by 24 to 30 inches wide

Fern-shaped plants feature large, glossy green leaves year-round

All-day shade or partial shade; protect from hot afternoon sun

Requires well-drained soil; amend soil with plenty of organic matter

Good choice for filling shady beds, growing in front of taller plants, adding to shady courtyards, entries, and niches; fine for confined spaces if drainage is good

Pairs well with daffodil, rhododendron, bleeding heart, Japanese maple, periwinkle, Pinxterbloom azalea, Lenten rose, mondo grass, dead nettle, star magnolia, bluestar, Spanish bluebell, windflower, leatherleaf mahonia, aucuba, and fothergilla

Zones 8–9, grow in sheltered areas in zone 7

Holly fern isn't a feathery thing that fades away. Plants grow nearly 2 feet tall and evergreen leaflets are large enough to fill beds with their presence.
Photo courtesy of Magnolia Gardens Nursery

23

(A) Holly fern is living proof that eye-catching color isn't everything. This plant's glossy foliage reflects the low light of a shade garden, adding sparkle to shadowy beds.
(B) The bright green color of new growth darkens as foliage matures. *Photo courtesy of Magnolia Gardens Nursery*

EASY BEAUTY

If you've got a shady bed located beneath deciduous trees, you can combine holly ferns with daffodil bulbs. The daffodils will bloom when sunlight filters through the trees' bare branches in late winter or early spring. When daffodils finish flowering they wither away, but it is not a good idea to cut the fading foliage because it continues to feed the bulbs for some time. When grown together, holly fern makes the process neater by hiding spent daffodils with its glossy green leaves. After the trees grow leaves, their canopies will protect holly fern from summer sun. Once planted, this effortless display of flowers will repeat each spring. The only thing you'll have to do is remove fallen tree leaves from the holly ferns in autumn.

ment. Poor soil that is hard and compacted is not suitable for this plant. Neither is heavy clay soil that holds excessive amounts of water. If the soil in your garden is hopeless and you want to grow holly fern, building a raised bed is your best bet. You can fill the new bed with fertile soil instead of working amendments into existing soil. Raised beds improve drainage, too. Water can drain through the new soil down to the existing soil, allowing holly fern's roots to dry completely after absorbing water as needed.

It is wise to keep holly fern beds mulched to preserve moisture without the need for frequent watering. If you notice water standing around plants, cut back on your watering immediately or roots will rot. Newly planted holly ferns usually require supplemental moisture but you must let roots dry completely between waterings. When grown in a well-shaded area in good soil, holly fern requires little to no attention except during periods of prolonged drought. Established plants will let you know they are thirsty by sprawling pitifully on the ground. Give them a good soaking right away and they'll perk back up. If your holly fern is thriving, you can pretty much leave it alone, though it is a good idea to refresh mulch in spring and autumn.

Tucking a layer of mulch around the base of plants in autumn helps them withstand cold temperatures. An unusually harsh winter may knock holly fern back a bit, but healthy plants should recover in the spring. Wait until new growth appears before removing damaged, browned fronds. Cutting dead fronds too soon may encourage tender new growth to emerge too early, resulting in additional freeze damage. You can occasionally prune away dead fronds during the warm months to tidy plants if you're so inclined, but there's no need to ever cut green plants back to the ground.

It's good to know that new growth on holly fern is a yellowish green. Foliage darkens to forest green as it ages. However, if you notice mature leaves that are pale, give plants a pick-me-up with an application or two of liquid fish emulsion.

BEDDING PLANTS: PERENNIALS

Hosta

Hosta species

Also sold as plantain lily, August lily, funkia

Don't believe the nay-sayers who claim that hostas can't be grown in the South. We can grow hostas in the South. We just can't grow *all kinds* of hostas in the South. We also can't grow hostas within reach of afternoon sun—and rarely will these lovely perennials thrive out of reach of a hose or sprinkler. But hostas we can grow.

With thousands of named selections available, hosta catalogs are filled with plants that don't thrive in the warm zones, so arm yourself with a little information before placing orders. Blue-leaved varieties perform poorly in the South. They need a longer winter's sleep than our mild climate can provide, and summer heat seems to melt the blue waxy substance right off the leaves. Miniature hostas have shallow roots that may not go far enough below the over-warmed top layer of soil in summer, making them poor choices for growing in our region as well.

But there are plenty of lovely hostas suitable for Southern gardens and choosing the right hosta is half the battle. For starters, there are fragrant hostas, which are all members or hybrids of the species *Hosta plantaginea*. Also known as plantain lilies, fragrant hostas have a temperament that's opposite of the blue-leaved varieties. Fragrant hostas can get by with a shorter period of dormancy and they require a longer growing season. They tend to sprout early in an attempt to get as much growing in as possible each year. This puts them in the off-limits category for gardens in colder regions and makes them well suited to Southern landscapes. *Hosta plantaginea* selections come in a range of leaf colors—greens, golds, and creamy highlights—but not true blue. White, sweetly scented flowers appear in multiples on long stalks called scapes in summer and are the largest blooms of all hostas.

GETTING ACQUAINTED

Perennial bedding plant

Sizes vary per selection; many hosta leaf clumps are under 2.5 feet high, though flower spikes are taller

Foliage colors vary greatly; flowers range from white to shades of purple

Slow rate of growth

Partial shade to mostly shady; protect from afternoon sun in summer

Moist, fertile soil that's well drained is best; established plants tolerate drier soil; not for soils that are wet, compacted, or highly alkaline

Good choice for moist, shady beds in formal or informal landscapes, entries, courtyards, and raised beds; fill beds or border the bedline; grow in masses or tucked here and there

Pairs well with daffodil, astilbe, foamflower, bleeding heart, bluestar, Japanese maple, rhododendron, hydrangeas, Virginia bluebell, trillium, caladium, periwinkle, impatiens, smilax, Japanese kerria, mondo grass, Lenten rose, liriope, celandine poppy, Japanese painted fern, Solomon's seal, star magnolia, dead nettle, aucuba, Virginia sweetspire, windflower, redbud, melampodium, Pinxterbloom azalea, and spring-blooming bulbs

Zones 3–9; not for frost-free areas

Yellow-tinted hostas fare much better in the South than the blue-leaved varieties.

HOSTAS FOR THE SOUTH

FRAGRANT HOSTAS: WHITE TO PALEST LAVENDER FLOWERS

SHADES OF GREEN, INCLUDING LIME AND YELLOWISH GREEN: *Hosta plantaginea*, 'Austin Dickinson', 'Honeybells', 'Royal Standard', 'Sweet Susan', 'Invincible', 'Guacamole', 'Fried Green Tomatoes', 'Rippled Honey', 'Tortilla Chip', 'Avocado', 'Old Faithful'

'Sum and Substance'

VARIEGATED WITH GREEN, WHITE, CREAM: 'Sugar and Cream', 'Savannah', 'Fragrant Dream', 'Summer Fragrance', 'So Sweet', 'Frozen Margarita'

YELLOW TO GOLD, SOLID OR VARIEGATED: 'Paradigm', 'Fragrant Bouquet', 'Fried Bananas'

NONFRAGRANT HOSTAS: LAVENDER TO PURPLE FLOWERS

SHADES OF GREEN, INCLUDING LIME AND YELLOWISH GREEN: *Hosta ventricosa*, 'Lancifolia', 'Golden Tiara', 'Sum and Substance', 'Gold Edger', 'August Moon'

VARIEGATED: GREEN, WHITE, CREAM: *H. ventricosa* 'Aureomarginata', 'Diamond Tiara', 'Sundance', 'Enterprise'

YELLOW TO GOLD, SOLID OR VARIEGATED: 'Captain Kirk', 'Gold Standard', 'Abba Dabba Do', 'Revolution', 'Squash Casserole'

HOSTA SHOPPING TIPS

Many of the hostas on the market will not thrive in Southern garden conditions, so make a wish list before you shop. Just because a local nursery or home center carries a certain hosta, it doesn't mean that it is the right plant for your area. Fortunately, you don't have to master much botanical Latin to buy a hosta you like that will also like your garden.

As a rule of thumb, avoid hostas with blue or blue-green foliage and stick to greens, yellows, and white-trimmed leaves instead. The brighter the leaf color, the more sun the hosta can take. Read the plant tag. Any hosta that's listed as fragrant, *plantaginea*, plantain lily, or August lily is a good choice; these clues indicate plants are heat-tolerant, fragrant hostas.

Finger the foliage before you buy. The thicker the leaf, the tougher the plant. Snails and slugs love to munch holes in thin-leaved hostas, so buy the thick-leaved selections. (Slugs and snails thrive in hot, humid climates; these slimy nuisances can be severely problematic in the lower, hotter zones of the South.) Lastly, learn from others. The named selections listed above are renowned for their reliability in Southern landscapes. To view photos, go to www.hostalibrary.org.

A

B

Although fragrant hostas are generally considered by hosta fanatics—I meant to say experts—to be the most heat tolerant of hostas, I personally find *Hosta ventricosa* hard to beat. The dark green, leathery leaves aren't showy compared to fancier selections, but there's something to be said for the lushness of a plant that stays richly green right through summer's heat. What it lacks in pizzazz, this hosta makes up for in durability. *Hosta ventricosa* isn't nearly as sun shy as a lot of other hostas, and it is not very picky about soil or water, either. A few transplants from a neighbor's garden have yielded hundreds of plants that now carpet several partially shaded beds in my upper zone 8 garden. I don't fuss over them, never fertilize, and rarely water. But I do leave spent flowers on their stalks

C

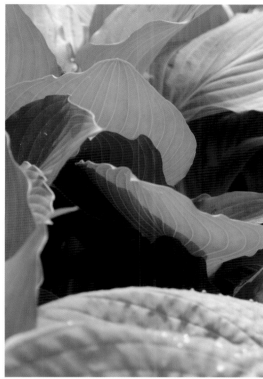

D

E

F

G

(A) Hostas are the perfect choice for bordering lawns grown in partial shade.

(B) When shaded from afternoon sun and grown in average garden soil, *Hosta ventricosa* becomes quite drought tolerant and truly maintenance-free. This hosta tolerates heat, humidity, drought, clay, sand, and even a little alkalinity better than most hostas do.

(C) Showy purple flower spikes top clumps of *Hosta ventricosa* foliage in summer.

(D) There's no pattern on *Hosta ventricosa* leaves, but lush greenery is welcome in garden beds.

(E) The buds of *Hosta ventricosa* are purple.

(F) Bell-shaped *Hosta ventricosa* blooms will set seed if you let pods dry on stalks after flowering finishes. You'll end up with all the green hostas you want.

(G) Variegated hosta lights up the shade. Big, coarse-textured leaves contrast well with more feathery foliage.

MAKING MORE PLANTS

Dividing thick, mature clumps of hostas in early spring is a reliable way of increasing your hosta population. Rinse cutting utensil with a solution of water and 10% household bleach before and after use. Dig rootballs, rinse them, and hack off a pie-shaped slice of the plant, including roots. Replant old and new plants. Water divided plants regularly throughout their first hot season.

FEEDING HOSTAS

Avoid using high-nitrogen fertilizer on hostas, as stems and leaves can become weak, mushy, and prone to problems. Instead, feed plants in spring with a balanced slow-release fertilizer.

well into the winter. *Hosta ventricosa* has a delightful habit of producing seedlings that look just like the parent. Of all the hostas in the horticultural world, it is the only one that can make this claim. Letting these hostas go to seed is well worth ignoring dead stalks in autumn. Summer flowers give way to pods that must ripen and dry in place. Most seeds will scatter by themselves, but you can aid the process by shaking out the black seeds once they're visible in the split pod. That's all you do. You'll have baby green hostas out your ears the following spring.

Though these true-to-seed plants are a different species from the fragrant *Hosta plantaginea*, or plantain lilies, *H. ventricosa* and selections are sometimes called blue plantain lilies. The blue in the name refers to the purple flowers, not to the foliage. An obsolete name for these sturdy, old-fashioned favorites is funkia. Though *H. ventricosa* is solid green, the leaves are pleasantly shiny. If that's too plain for your taste, try *Hosta ventricosa* 'Aureomarginata', or variegated blue plantain lily. Though you won't get seedlings, this hosta combines attractive green-and-cream foliage with superior Southern durability.

You may see the phrase "sun tolerant" listed on the plant tags of some hostas. While its true that all hostas need some sun to thrive—and those with variegated leaves need a little more to maintain their colorful foliage—no hosta should be planted in direct sun in the South. The closer to the equator you get, the hotter the sun is and the more quickly hostas will be damaged by it. It is wise to protect all hostas from afternoon sun in the South, regardless of what the plant tag claims. When growers say a hosta will grow in full sun, go ahead and translate that to mean partial sun—and rays should reach hostas only during the first part of the day. Noonday, afternoon, and evening sun are taboo for hostas in our region. There are always a few exceptions, such as gardens grown at higher elevations, but chances are the only sunlight hostas can handle in your landscape is the kind that comes from the east in the morning. Even then, it is a good idea if the sunlight is somewhat filtered for a dappled effect.

Most hostas are thirsty plants because water transpires from their large leaves quickly. The natural Asian habitats of hostas receive high amounts of annual rainfall. Our region does, too, but it is often uneven: deluge followed by drought. Hostas prefer to be kept evenly moist. Wet winter soil isn't good for them, either. Happily, all this can be overcome with some effort on your part. Except for *Hosta ventricosa*, most hostas require regular water in spring and autumn while they're actively growing. An inch of water per week per plant, whether from rainfall, the hose, or a sprinkler system, is advisable. It is best to avoid letting roots dry completely between waterings, but if you do upon occasion, it may merely slow the plant's growth. Morning is the best time to water because hydrated hostas are ready to face the heat of the day. Early watering also enables leaves to dry, which discourages slugs.

Keep in mind that it is possible to overwater your hostas and that's as bad as letting them become dry. You'll be less inclined to water too much

in an attempt to keep your hostas happy if you've equipped the soil to help get the moisture right. When planting just about any hosta, mix your native soil with plenty of peat, compost, large-particle organic matter (such as pine bark), and sand (unless your soil is naturally sandy). These amendments will help provide nutrients and retain moisture while also permitting intense amounts of water to drain away from roots. Plentiful water is necessary for most hostas to thrive, but good drainage is equally important to prevent crown rot and mushy roots. Adequate drainage becomes an even more significant requirement in areas that receive large amounts of winter precipitation.

Though it seems like a silly waste of effort, it is best to dig holes for hostas about 3 feet wide and 1 foot or more deep, regardless of how small the plant is at the time. After you've prepared a lush soil mixture, fill the hole with enough soil to make your unpotted hosta protrude just slightly. After checking the hosta's position, remove the plant and fill the hole with several inches of water. Put the hosta back in place and fill around it with soil mixture and a small dose of slow-release fertilizer per the package direc-

Hostas keep the ground plane lush in shady planting compositions.

HOSTA

tions. As the water seeps into pores in the new soil, the mixture will settle, bringing your plant down to its proper level. Mulch around the hosta but keep mulch away from stems. Water the newly situated plant with a trickling hose aimed at the soil beneath the leaves.

The above instructions describe hosta planting at its best. The farther south you live, the more important it becomes to do the job correctly. But you don't have to go too far north to cheat a little. If your soil is somewhat rich or woodsy and drains fairly well, you can wimp out some on the planting effort. However, you still must adhere to the rule about selecting locations shaded from afternoon summer sun—that one really is nonnegotiable in our climate. But if you choose tough hostas, you can ease up on watering once plants become well established in your garden.

Japanese Painted Fern

Athyrium niponicum 'Pictum'

May be sold as *Athyrium goeringianum* 'Pictum' or 'Metallicum'

Some plant names leave you scratching your head in wonder. My enjoyment of bloody cranesbill—a lovely little bloomer—will be forever marred by my aversion to its name. On the other end of the spectrum are plants with logical monikers that are easy to remember because they describe their subject so well. Japanese painted fern belongs to the latter club. It certainly looks like a plant that would be at home in a Japanese-themed garden. It looks painted, too—green fronds generously splashed with silver are trimmed with purplish midribs and stems. The color scheme of this imported perennial makes it noticeable enough to serve as an accent, yet subtle enough to be stylish instead of flashy.

Japanese painted ferns grow slowly, so you'll rarely find them on the bargain table. However, you can start with a handful of these perennials and create an effective accent via strategic placement. Set Japanese painted ferns in odd-numbered groupings in prominent spots. They show off nicely beside stones, sculpture, and benches. They're also good choices for cultivating in damp soil near water, so plant them in shady locations beside ponds, fountains, waterfalls, and streams. Painted ferns that are grown in naturally moist soil rarely require any attention beyond occasional watering during droughts. When they're kept happily moist, these ferns will eventually spread.

If you've got the right conditions—moist, fertile soil and shade—growing Japanese painted fern is quite easy. If you don't, bypass this plant unless you're prepared to make an effort to keep roots watered. Japanese painted fern won't thrive in sun, dry soil, or extremely alkaline areas (soils with very high pH, often caused by a limestone or chalky base). Clay soils that are suitably moist and shaded can be improved by working chunky

GETTING ACQUAINTED

Perennial bedding plant

12 to 18 inches high and wide

Green foliage bears silvery stripes with purplish highlights

Slow rate of growth

All-day shade, filtered shade, afternoon shade; limited morning sun is okay

Fertile soil that's moist or wet; not for poor, dry soil or highly alkaline soil (slightly alkaline is fine)

Good choice for growing in masses or tucking here and there in shady beds, along pathways, beside shaded patios, benches, ponds, fountains, and streams; adapts well to narrow spaces; good for entries and courtyards

Pairs well with astilbe, foamflower, Solomon's seal, hosta, Japanese maple, caladium, celandine poppy, bluebells, hydrangeas, trillium, dead nettle, bleeding heart, Lenten rose, mondo grass, windflower, wishbone flower, rhododendron, star magnolia, redbud, impatiens, melampodium, Pinxterbloom azalea, and other ferns

Zones 4–8

New fronds of Japanese painted fern start off light green and gain their distinctive coloration as they mature. *Photo courtesy of Greenwood Nursery*

Japanese painted ferns are slow to appear in spring, but they're worth the wait. You can set a few ferns in among other low-growing bedding plants as subtle accents. Or, plant a patch of them and let ferns spread to create a mass of fronds.
Photo courtesy of The Crownsville Nursery

organic matter, such as leaf humus or compost, into beds prior to planting. The better the soil, the less watering you'll need to do to grow lush ferns.

Japanese painted ferns that receive too much direct, hot sunshine will require a lot of supplemental water. It is a good idea to dig up and move plants that get blasted by summer afternoon sun or they'll end up with crispy fronds. But you needn't avoid the sun altogether. That's because all-day shade erases some of the silvery painted quality of the foliage. A little dappled sunlight throughout the day or morning rays from the east will keep colors strong without scorching the fronds.

Japanese painted ferns only grow a foot or so high, making it important to position these pretty little plants where you can enjoy them up close. You'll waste your money if you plant them in the background, where they'll recede into the shadows or become blocked from view by taller plants. Hostas make an excellent companion as long as larger selections are planted behind Japanese painted fern.

NAMED SELECTIONS

'BURGUNDY LACE': showy purple parts
'URSULA'S RED': new growth is wine colored
SILVER FALLS®: showy silvery tones intensify
    as leaves mature; red veins

TUCKING THEM IN

Mulch helps preserve moisture and keeps soil temperatures cooler. Add organic mulch to painted fern beds in spring and autumn by tucking it around stems. Foliage usually dies back completely in winter, but painted fern roots are quite cold hardy. You can count on fresh fronds to sprout in the spring. A loose mulch, such as pine straw, makes it easy for new growth to emerge.

Lenten Rose

Helleborus orientalis

Also sold as hellebore, *Helleborus* x *hybridus*

I
f you want flowers that last for at least two months, foliage that stays green year-round, and blooming that begins by February and won't flinch in snow, then perhaps you're in the market for a bouquet of plastic flowers. Not to your taste? Then try Lenten rose. It offers all of the above and more.

Lenten roses aren't roses—they're in the buttercup family. Also called hellebores, Lenten roses are sturdy, evergreen perennials that thrive in well-drained, humus-rich soil. Though they're imports to our country, these old-fashioned favorites are at home in woodland settings and show off nicely beside early-spring wildflowers. Mounds of foliage stay under 2 feet tall, widening as plants age. Flowers are large, somewhat cupped, and grow nestled against leathery, dark green leaves. In cooler climates, blooming occurs in the weeks prior to Easter; the plant's name refers to the Lenten season. In the South, flowers open sooner, usually sometime in February or perhaps as early as January. Cold snaps don't damage blossoms or leaves, though plants should be sheltered from harsh, shredding winds.

Species Lenten roses are available with flowers that are white, cream, greenish pink, rose, and speckled variations of these themes. Hybridizing the *Helleborus* genus has become something of a passion among devotees of this perennial. As a result, newly named selections appear on the market every year. Because seeds are frequently untrue to the parent plant's characteristics, it is best to buy potted Lenten roses that have been propagated from cuttings. Creative breeding has yielded plants boasting a wide range of flower colors and shapes. Blossoms of hybrids come in yellow, lime green, white, cream, pink, rose, plum, combinations of these hues, and even black. The hybrids include simple flowers resembling five-pointed stars, ruffled double blooms that bear

GETTING ACQUAINTED

Perennial bedding plant

18 to 24 inches high and 24 to 30 inches wide

Large nodding flowers bloom in early spring, opening in shades of pale green to white to rose; many hybrids available in different shades and flower shapes

Slow rate of growth

Resistant to insects and disease

Partial shade to all-day shade; blooms best with some sun in late winter and early spring, but protect from summer sun

Rich, woodsy soil, moist to dry; not for soil that's compacted or wet

Good choice for woodland gardens, beds that are shady and moist, natural areas, along paths, confined spaces with good drainage, raised beds, and slopes

Pairs well with foamflower, bluestar, celandine poppy, dogwood, redbud, Spanish bluebell, Solomon's seal, Japanese maple, trillium, star magnolia, hydrangeas, daffodil, redbud, rhododendron, Pinxterbloom azalea, bluebells, holly fern, hosta, mondo grass, littleleaf periwinkle, windflower, melampodium, Virginia sweetspire, Japanese painted fern, other ferns and spring-blooming bulbs

Zones 4–8

Lenten roses are also known as hellebores. They bloom in late winter.

A

B

some semblance to roses, and anemone-style flowers that combine characteristics. The choices are overwhelming, so buy your plants in bloom to see what you're getting.

Whether you're planting the species Lenten rose or one of the newer hybrids, you'll need to find a spot that's at least partially shaded. All-day summer shade is recommended for growing Lenten rose in gardens in lower zone 8. From upper zone 8 to zone 4, any site that's protected from afternoon sun in the summer will do. Plants will thrive in all-day shade, dappled shade throughout the day, or summertime morning sun followed by afternoon shade.

Lenten roses want good, rich soil that drains well. Heavy clay should be amended with gypsum or sand plus chunky compost prior to planting. Fertile, woodsy soil is excellent. Average garden soil can be improved with generous doses of decayed organic matter. If water doesn't flow freely through your soil, grow Lenten roses on slopes or behind retaining walls or build a raised bed to improve drainage. Lenten rose roots that stay wet will rot.

Set new plants in beds so that surface of the soil from the nursery container is level with the adjacent bedding soil. Plants set too deeply will eventually die. Mulch Lenten roses well to keep roots cool and moist, but not wet. Water these plants regularly throughout their first spring and summer, but always let roots dry out between waterings. Reduce watering in autumn, tapering off for winter. After a good stand of roots are established, Lenten roses become remarkably drought tolerant if shade is adequate. Take care not to overwater these perennials. They need far less water than grass or annuals, so adjust sprinklers accordingly.

Once you have Lenten roses growing in your garden, they require little maintenance. Supplemental watering will rarely be necessary outside of

c

drought conditions. Allow Lenten roses to develop thick clumps. Don't
dig up plants and divide them; just let them grow. In good soil and shade,
they'll spread naturally but not aggressively. Always take care to prevent
mulch and fallen leaves from burying your Lenten roses deeper than you
originally planted them. Even after years of success in the same spot, a
healthy plant will decline and die if stems can't access air to stay dry or if
roots remain wet. Spreading a 3-inch-thick layer of compost on the soil
beneath plants—a practice known as topdressing—will provide nutrients
and help preserve moisture without overwatering. Topdressing is needed
just once a year. Keep compost away from stems. If you can bring yourself
to do it, borrow a trick from professional growers and shear big plants back
gently in late winter when flowers first begin to appear. Cut stems back
to just above the blossoms. You'll be amazed at the flush of growth that
results to compliment a full show of flowers.

(A) The nodding flowers of *Helleborus orientalis*
are best seen if these short perennials are planted
close to eye level. Raised beds, slopes, and spots
behind retaining walls are ideal for viewing.
(B) Lenten roses have been hybridized to include a
wide range of flower colors and shapes. Blossoms
are available in pink, white, plum, rose, lime, yellow,
and speckled variations.
(C) Large, evergreen leaves keep these plants
attractive year-round. Lenten roses grow well near
most trees, but keep them away from the shallow
roots of maples.

Polygonatum species

Solomon's Seal

GETTING ACQUAINTED

Perennial bedding plant

Size varies per selection from 1 to 7 feet high and 1 to 3 feet wide

Solid green leaves or foliage variegated with cream; small flowers range from greenish cream to white

Moderate to slow rate of growth

Resistant to insects and disease

All-day shade to partial shade

Fertile soil; moist soil is best but plants adapt well to dry conditions; not for compacted soil; add compost to sandy soil prior to planting

Good choice for narrow spaces, including shaded beds beside walls, patios, and walkways; add to shade gardens, wildflower gardens, rock gardens, natural areas, trails, and woodland gardens; useful in both formal and informal designs

Pairs well with bleeding heart, trillium, bluestar, astilbe, star magnolia, hosta, mondo grass, Japanese painted fern, fothergilla, Virginia bluebell, rhododendron, Japanese maple, hydrangeas, Virginia sweetspire, smilax, celandine poppy, foamflower, pieris, periwinkle, climbing hydrangea, Pinxterbloom azalea, red buckeye, and Lenten rose

Zones 3–9

Solomon's seal is an easy perennial for shade.

It is a wise gardener who grows Solomon's seal. This perennial shines in the shade, grows in moist or dry soil, and is maintenance-free. It is long-lived and spreads at a modest pace to develop colonies that fill shadowy beds. Plants grow happily in all-day shade or partial shade. Heat, cold, and insects are no problem.

There are many varieties of Solomon's seal, including an all-green native plant and several variegated *Polygonatum* species from Asia. The cream-and-green color schemes of the imports are particularly valuable for brightening shady beds. The fat, egg-shaped leaves zigzag their way up stalks, almost paired but not quite. Each green leaf bears delicate brushstrokes of ivory. This is variegation at it is finest.

The stalks of Solomon's seal have no branches but they're not missed. Each stalk shoots up vertically from the ground and then arches over in an elegant sweeping fashion. Multiple stalks stand shoulder to shoulder, spilling their bold leaves together. Bell-shaped blossoms dangle on slender stems from the undersides of mature stalks in mid to late spring. The flowers are borne on the bowed parts of stalks, beneath the leaves, and range from greenish cream to white.

Though the dainty blossoms are enchanting, the real merit of Solomon's seal is its bold, architectural presence and coarse texture, which is a designer's way of saying that the plant's shape and leaf size are noticeable and attractive. The broad leaves contrast beautifully with fine-textured plants that thrive in shade, including ferns, mondo grass, astilbe, bleeding heart, and foamflower. Grow one or more of these delicate plants intermingled with a Solomon's seal for a head-turning combination. When this perennial is grown in a partially shaded bed that receives a good bit of winter sunlight, you can plant daffodils and Solomon's seal together. The bulbs will bloom before the large perennial is conspicuous and provide an early show.

A

B

C

Later, the Solomon's seal will take the stage and help hide fading daffodil foliage.

Solomon's seal seeds are notoriously difficult to germinate, so start with live plants or rhizomes. These thick, fleshy roots need only to be buried in a few inches of soil, so it is easy to give them the good stuff. This perennial will adapt to average garden soil and dry conditions, but it's best to start it off in a bed of moist soil enriched with decaying leaves or compost. Lay rhizomes horizontally; if there's a stalk attached, prop it up or trim it to prevent plants from tipping over and uprooting. Water gently and add a few inches of lush organic mulch, such as more rotting leaves. You can

(A) The flowers of Solomon's seal are hung on long stems from the undersides of graceful stalks.
(B) Variegated Solomon's seal has the added benefit of leaves that turn lemon yellow in autumn while retaining their white edges.
(C) Blue-black berries dangle from arching stems of the taller selections of Solomon's seal in autumn.

NAME GAME

Solomon's seal belongs to a complicated genus. It is rare to find two horticultural-ists who agree on which species and subspecies delineate different plants and which are merely aliases of the same plant. Your best bet is to read plant tags and nursery descriptions carefully to get what you want; growers are probably describing the characteristics of their plants accurately, even if the Latin name may be questionable. If you're shopping for a wildflower garden, keep in mind that native Solomon's seal only comes with plain green leaves. The variegated plants are imports. Use the following as a guide when untangling *Polygonatum* nomenclature.

POLYGONATUM BIFLORUM: green leaves and stalks, 1 to 3 feet high, upright stalks are noticeable, may be sold as false Solomon's seal, native Solomon's seal, or smooth Solomon's seal

False Solomon's seal is the species *Polygonatum biflorum*. This perennial is native and does not have striped leaves. Red berries are borne in clusters on the tips of stalks.

POLYGONATUM COMMUTATUM: green leaves and stalks, 3 to 7 feet high, upright stalks are noticeable; may be sold as great Solomon's seal

The native green-leaved *Polygonatum commutatum* gets taller than the selections with variegated foliage.

POLYGONATUM MULTIFLO-RUM 'VARIEGATUM': cream-and-green leaves on reddish stalks, under 2 feet high, appears flatter because you look down on leaves, may be sold as variegated Solomon's seal

Variegated Solomon's seal, *Polygonatum multiflorum* 'Variegatum', is a popular choice among gardeners. Reddish stalks are an identifying characteristic.

POLYGONATUM ODORATUM 'VARIEGATUM': cream-and-green leaves on green stalks, 2 to 3 feet high, upright stalks are noticeable; also sold as variegated Solomon's seal, varie-gated Japanese Solomon's Seal, *Polygonatum odoratum* var. *thunbergii* 'Variegatum', or *Polygonatum japonicum* 'Variegatum'

Like *Polygonatum multiflorum* 'Variegatum'. *P. odoratum* 'Variegatum' is also called varie-gated Solomon's seal, but it has green stalks that grow upright instead of outward.

snap larger rhizomes into smaller pieces and spread them apart to start multiple plants.

If you're digging plants from an established colony of Solomon's seal, scrape away soil to expose the roots of plants along an outer edge of the group. Separate a plant at the roots with the shovel blade and scoop up the entire plant along with a good amount of soil. Replant in a prepared bed right away or move to a pot of soil for transporting elsewhere. If you find that the rhizomes are knotted and thick, you may have to snap them apart or even hack off one or two plants with a clean pruning saw. Replant any unearthed roots that you don't intend to move. Always position Solomon's seal where it will be sheltered from afternoon sun. Morning sun-light or dappled sunlight is fine, as is no direct sunlight at all, but hot western rays can scorch leaves and weaken this perennial.

It's easier to separate rhizomes from existing colonies without damaging leaves if you do it in early spring while stalks are still short. Dividing Solomon's seal isn't a requirement to keep plants vigorous—do it only to make baby plants. If you want, you may skip the digging and dividing by simply adding one or two of these perennials to a bed and letting them spread on their own. Autumn is the best time to set out rhizomes or container-grown plants, but you can add them to your garden in spring, too. Solomon's seals started in spring will require a little more water during their first hot season than plants started the previous autumn.

Solomon's seal grown in moist, fertile soil will spread more quickly than plants grown in dry soil. But less-aggressive growth is a small price to pay for filling those difficult dry shade spots near tree roots. Solomon's seal is so adaptable, it will even grown beneath maples, which are notorious for their greedy, shallow roots. Once established, Solomon's seals growing in dry soil rarely need watering. You really can get this plant going and then forget about it.

Flowers fade away in summer, but foliage stays lush and full. Dangling green berries take the flowers' places, and by autumn the fruit is blue-black. Solomon's seals leaves turn a pretty lemon yellow in autumn. The creamy streaks of variegated *Polygonatum* species fade lighter, so autumn foliage on these plants combines yellow and white attractively on each leaf. The native green-leafed Solomon's seal turns yellow-green in autumn. Leaves and stalks eventually die away. Allow fallen leaves from trees to collect on the bed where your Solomon's seal grows. The leaves will decay and form natural mulch. New shoots come back better than ever each spring, year after year.

Hyacinthoides hispanica

Also sold as *Scilla hispanica, Scilla campanulata, Endymion hispanicus*

GETTING ACQUAINTED

Perennial bedding plant

12 to 18 inches high and wide; forms spreading clumps

Light blue, bell-shaped flowers are borne on short stalks above leaves in midspring

Moderate rate of growth

Resistant to insects and disease

Nonnative; may be invasive in frost-free areas

Partial shade to all-day shade

Any well-drained soil, including soil that's poor and dry; not for wet soil; tolerates drought and dry sandy soil

Good choice for woodland gardens, natural areas, shady beds, tucked in front of taller plants, mixed with groundcover. Pretty beside entries, in courtyards, and in rock gardens. Good filler for empty annual beds.

Pairs well with periwinkle, daffodil, Japanese painted fern, bluestar, holly fern, Pinxterbloom azalea, star magnolia, hydrangeas, Lenten rose, redbud, camellia, dead nettle, gooseneck loosestrife, beautyberry, oakleaf hydrangea, windflower, and Japanese kerria

Zones 4–9

Spanish bluebell is one of those perennials that has little or no presence for much of the year, but reappears to bloom beautifully each spring. Though the period of bloom is brief, plants are long-lived and flower faithfully.

Spanish Bluebell

There's a reason the Spanish bluebell is a common inhabitant of old gardens. A plant this pretty found itself welcome; a plant this tough decided to stay and multiply. All you really need to grow Spanish bluebells in your own garden is some shade and soil that drains well. Plant the little bulbs and forget about them. It's that easy. You'll enjoy effortless blossoms for years.

Clumps of glossy, narrow foliage appear out of nowhere in early spring. Each clump produces numerous stalks extending 6 to 10 inches above the leaves. By the time warm days are here to stay, Spanish bluebells are in

bloom. Each green stem bears nodding flowers that are blue to lavender-blue. The bell-shaped blossoms must have made naming this plant easy. Cut flowers make sweet, simple arrangements in small bottles or vases filled with water.

Spanish bluebells aren't picky about sun and shade. They thrive in partial shade, but all-day dappled shade or a half-day's worth of shade are also fine. Some sun promotes flowering but blossom colors may fade when grown in full sun all day long. Deeply shaded spots are fine for Spanish bluebells, too. They'll bloom valiantly in the shadows, though perhaps not quite as prolifically. But remember, many of the spots in your landscape that you consider shady will actually receive a good bit of sun in late winter and early spring before tree canopies are in leaf. Such areas are ideal for growing Spanish bluebells. You can even plant these bulbs among tree roots. These pretty perennials will grow in dry shade where fussier plants won't.

You can plant the bulbs any time you can find them for sale, as long as the temperature is well above freezing. Spanish bluebell bulbs like to be planted quite a bit deeper than many other bulbs. Dig a hole that's

A   B   C

about 6 inches deep and wide. Set bulbs pointy-end-up and cover with a mixture of native soil and sand; omit the sand if your soil is naturally well drained. Planted bulbs should sit 4 to 5 inches deep. Set two or three bulbs together in each hole to get a cluster of plants growing. Water thoroughly once or twice. Bulbs will produce roots in autumn and leaves the next spring.

As they mature, bulbs will enlarge and produce bulblets that cling to the parent plant by the roots. If you know someone who has Spanish bluebells to share, you can dig up bulbs and move them to your own garden. Be forewarned, though, the bulbs sink deep and don't come up easily. As often as not, you'll end up slicing bulbs to pieces with the shovel blade.

The sandier your soil is, the more quickly Spanish bluebells will multiply and spread—so make sure you want them before you add them to your garden. Plants grown in dense soil will also bloom reliably each spring as long as water isn't held around the bulbs, causing them to rot. Though Spanish bluebells thrive in the shade, they really aren't harmed by summer sun because they've already gone dormant by the time hot days roll around. After flowering, Spanish bluebells fade away entirely. If you're planning to dig up bulbs for transplanting, it is best to do so after blooming but before clumps disappear entirely for the remainder of the year.

After you've forgotten all about them, your Spanish bluebells will reappear the following spring and bloom heartily again. There's no need to fertilize, divide, spray, or even water them. Just enjoy.

(A) This appealing little perennial is amazingly easy to grow. Spanish bluebell thrives in dry soil, so you can plant it near tree roots.
(B) The blossoms of Spanish bluebell are borne on stalks held about the strappy foliage. Flowers open from the bottom of the stalks upward.
(C) Delicate bell-shaped blooms make this plant loveable, but be aware that in frost-free areas with loose soil, Spanish bluebells will spread far and wide.

SPANISH BLUEBELL

NAMED SELECTIONS

Unless identified by a name other than *Hyacinthoides hispanica*, Spanish bluebells have light blue flowers. These cultivars bloom in other hues.

'QUEEN OF PINKS': lilac-pink
'WHITE CITY': snowy white
'EXCELSIOR': deep blue

Trillium sessile

Also sold as toadshade, wakerobin, toadshade trillium, trinity plant, red or bronze trillium, *Trillium cuneatum*

GETTING ACQUAINTED

Perennial bedding plant

4 to 10 inches high; may appear as single plants a few inches wide or as spreading colonies several feet across

Showy foliage is marbled green and gray; flowers are maroon or yellow (*T. luteum*)

Slow rate of growth

Resistant to insects and disease

Native

All-day shade, partial shade

Fertile soil that's moist in spring; okay if soil is dry in summer; not for compacted soil

Good choice for moist, shady beds, wildflower gardens, rock gardens, woodland gardens, entries, narrow spaces, and for tucking at the feet of taller plants

Pairs well with Lenten rose, Virginia bluebell, astilbe, hosta, bleeding heart, foamflower, bluestar, star magnolia, Japanese maple, Japanese painted fern, Solomon's Seal, hydrangeas, Pinxterbloom azalea, rhododendron, celandine poppy, red buckeye, and various ferns

Zones 4–8

Look, don't pick. If you pick the stalk that bears foliage and flowers, you'll kill the trillium plant. And though it is not noticeable in the fresh air, trillium blossoms bear a fragrance that may be objectionable indoors.

Trillium

Somewhere along the way, gardeners got on a first name basis with this shy wildflower, so it's often sold as trillium. I prefer the name toadshade myself, as it is the perfect size to serve as a toad's parasol. You'll also find that many nurseries combine the names, selling plants as toadshade trillium. Others call it wakerobin.

The spring flowers of this native plant are small and maroon. The petals stand up straight and barely open. But the true beauty is in the combination of flower and foliage. This plant's species name is *sessile*, which means stemless, to describe the burgundy blossoms that squat right on top of three large leaves. Each leaf is egg-shaped and handsomely marbled with green and gray. They top an otherwise bare maroon stalk. Sometimes the triplet leaves are tinged with burgundy, as if to better complement the stalk and central flower.

From summer through winter, trilliums remain in hiding, existing merely as underground roots. They come out of seclusion in early to midspring. That's when stalks pop through fallen leaves and unfurl the distinctive foliage and flower combinations. In its natural setting, much of the forest floor around the trillium is still brown and gray at bloom time, making this wildflower's appearance all the more striking.

To add *Trillium sessile* to your garden, seek reputable specialty growers who cultivate native plants and wildflowers. Trilliums may be protected species in your area, and if they're not, they should be, so don't dig them from the woods. Because the seeds are notoriously difficult to germinate, buy live plants in containers. Midspring is the best time to plant trillium. Cover roots with 2 inches of moist, fertile soil and mulch around stems with decaying leaves. Keep new transplants watered until midsummer. Trillium enters dormancy during dry periods, so it will disappear when

A

B

C

heat and sun conspire to dry the upper layers of soil. This is normal, and plants reappear the following spring.

Trillium can grow in heavy all-day shade, dappled shade, or half-day's shade. Rich, moist soil enables plants to thrive in sunnier spots. In the South, hot afternoon sun is probably too taxing for trilliums except those growing in cool, mountainous areas, so provide shelter from western rays. The farther south you live, the more shade trilliums will require in your garden and the more watering you'll need to do in spring.

If fallen leaves have been allowed to decay instead of being raked away, the shadowy area beneath deciduous trees is ideal for growing trilliums. You can enrich less-than-perfect soil with compost, rotted leaves, or both; build raised beds if necessary to create a hospitable setting. Trilliums are lovely when grown along trails, in wildflower gardens, woodlands, and shady natural areas. This perennial combines well with other spring bloomers, such as Virginia bluebell and celandine poppy. Plants that show up later in the summer when trillium has gone to bed make good companions, too—astilbe, hostas, and ferns can hide its absence.

Once established, *Trillium sessile* is best left alone. In rich, woodsy soil that's moist in springtime, these wildflowers will eventually spread to form colonies. Only when you've got a good stand going should you can dig up plants in bloom to move elsewhere in your garden or to share with friends. Use a sharp shovel to separate roots. Scoop up an entire plant in a trowel full of soil, and replant in its new location as quickly as possible. Never attempt to divide an entire bed. Instead, dig offshoots on the edge of the colony, so you'll disturb fewer roots.

(A) The small sprout at the base of this pair of *Trillium sessile* stalks is evidence of the plants spreading to form a colony. Wait until there are plenty of plantlets before carefully digging the outer plants to move elsewhere.

(B) The large, marbled leaves of trilliums contrast well with delicate foliage. The feathery plant shown here is Dutchman's breeches, *Dicentra cucullaria*, a relative of bleeding heart and the yellow-flower trillium is *T. luteum*.

(C) *Trillium sessile* is sometimes called bronze trillium for the maroon to purple flowers that crown the foliage.

Yellow trillium (Trillium luteum) has lemony petals.

YELLOW TRILLIUM

Trillium luteum is quite similar to bronze trillium, but the central flower petals are pale yellow instead of maroon or bronze. The two species intermingle nicely, so you can grow them together to enjoy both colors.

TRILLIUM

Mertensia virginica

Also sold as lungwort, Virginia cowslip

Virginia Bluebell

GETTING ACQUAINTED

Perennial bedding plant

12 to 18 inches high and wide

Clusters of sky-blue flowers open from pink
buds in spring; each bell-shaped blossom is
about 1 inch long

Slow rate of growth

Native

Partial shade to all-day shade; protect from hot
afternoon sun

Rich, woodsy soil that's moist and well drained;
not for poor dry soil

Good choice for wildflower gardens, wooded
areas, and shady beds with good soil

Pairs well with bleeding heart, trillium, daffodil,
Japanese painted fern, astilbe, foamflower,
Solomon's seal, Japanese maple, hosta,
mondo grass, red buckeye, celandine poppy,
Lenten rose, ferns, and shade-loving sum-
mer annuals

Zones 3–8

Virginia bluebells are native wildflowers that
appear each spring.

Virginia bluebells bloom from early to midspring. It is an attractive process, one that starts with pink buds forming on the tips of plants. As buds open, they change from pink to blue, going through an in-between stage that's quite purplish. Blossoms mature at different rates, so it is not uncommon to enjoy all three colors at once on the same plant. The full-fledged flowers dangle downward like long, sky-blue bells, causing the tops of plants to arch gracefully. Blossoms bear a light, sweet scent, but it is rarely appreciated unless the plants are grown in quantity.

Unlike the Spanish bluebell, which is an import, the Virginia bluebell is native. It grows freely in moist woodlands of the eastern United States. You can cultivate it in your garden if you mimic this wildflower's natural habitat. Shade, fertile soil, ample moisture, and good drainage are what Virginia bluebells desire. They can grow in all-day shade, in afternoon shade with a few hours of morning sun, or in all-day dappled shade. Given the right conditions, these lovely plants will thrive and spread. Each spring will bring more plants and more flowers, though Virginia bluebells are not prone to overpopulate the way Spanish bluebells are when the latter is grown in its ideal setting.

Given less than perfect conditions, Virginia bluebells may bloom reliably each spring, but they'll probably fail to multiply or form large plants. They'll still be enjoyable even if they don't become widespread. But too much hot sun, drought, or standing water can kill Virginia bluebells. Poor soil will cause plants to decline. Unless your soil is naturally rich and woodsy, add plenty of compost, rotted leaves, or other organic matter to beds before planting these wildflowers. Such soil amendments will increase fertility and improve drainage, too. It is not a bad idea to mulch

A

B

around plants in spring with a thin topdressing of finely rotted compost, staying clear of stems.

Virginia bluebell leaves are light green and rounded. The coarse texture contrasts prettily with fine-textured foliage of other shade lovers such as astilbe and ferns. Like Spanish bluebells, Virginia bluebells are spring-blooming ephemerals, so their period of dormancy is induced by heat, not by cold. Foliage fades away sometime after flowering finishes, but don't cut the withered leaves because they're still producing foot for the roots. By midsummer, plants are pretty much gone from view. You can inter-plant Virginia bluebells with ferns, mondo grass, astilbe, and shade-loving annuals to camouflage blank spots left in beds by dormant bluebells, but take care to avoid disturbing the sleeping wildflowers. You'll get a fresh crop of blue flowers and light green foliage each spring.

(A) The flower buds of Virginia bluebell are pinkish purple.
(B) Some sky-blue flowers open while others are still in bud, providing a range of colors on each Virginia bluebell plant.

Anemone blanda

Also sold as anemone, Grecian windflower, Greek thimbleweed

GETTING ACQUAINTED

Perennial bedding plant

3 to 4 inches high by about 6 inches wide; flowers self-seed to form spreading carpets

Little daisylike flowers open in early spring in shades of blue, white, and pink

Moderate rate of growth

Tolerates cold

Partial shade; needs winter sun to bloom; all-day shade in summer is fine

Any well-drained soil

Good choice for woodland paths, shaded rock gardens, courtyards, and entries; tuck into mulched gaps in beds by setting windflowers in front of taller plants

Pairs well with daffodil, celandine poppy, astilbe, hosta, Spanish bluebell, Lenten rose, aucuba, Pinxterbloom azalea, Japanese maple, leatherleaf mahonia, oakleaf hydrangea, star magnolia, redbud, fothergilla, Japanese painted fern, holly fern, and bulbs that flower in early spring

Zones 4–8

Although commonly called windflowers, plant these delicate little perennials where they'll be sheltered from strong gusts.

Windflower

Windflower is a decorative detail, like colored sprinkles on cupcake frosting. This isn't one of those sturdy, problem-solving plants that you'll rely upon to anchor your landscape year-round. In fact, it is not even visible for a good part of the year. Windflowers are easy to omit, but include them if you can—there's a reason why those sprinkled cupcakes are always the first to go. Sometimes, pure prettiness is justification enough.

Only 3 to 4 inches high, windflowers are what I call "little growies." They're lovely tucked here and there or grown together as a spreading carpet. Though windflowers would be pretty any time of year, these wee perennials would be easy to overlook if they bloomed on a schedule more popular with other flowers. But clever little windflowers open early, showing off as bright dabs of color in the still-brown landscape. They pop out of bare ground when spring is still a young and hesitant season. Delicate green leaves unfold first, and the flowers soon follow. Each bloom is held on its own short stem just above a low mound of tender foliage. Each mounding plant produces multiple flowers. The effect is simple and sweet.

Shades of blue, lavender, and violet are most the common blossom colors, but they're definitely not commonplace. For one thing, the horticultural world is filled with warm colors but cool blues are a little more elusive. For another, the windflower is an underused perennial, not as widely planted as it should be considering its low maintenance status. In addition to blue-to-purple hues, windflowers are available with white blossoms as well as a range of pinks. Flowers close when the sun goes down.

Windflowers prefer cool soil, but they require sun to bloom. Meeting such needs isn't nearly as tricky as it sounds, thanks to this perennial's

A

B

(A) 'White Splendour' windflower is stunning beside miniature red tulips.
(B) Windflower buds open as cup-shaped blossoms that flatten like little daises.

habit of blooming early. Select a spot that's under bare branches in winter for adequate early-spring sunlight. When those same branches develop leaves later in the season, the windflowers growing beneath them will have finished flowering and will be ready to rest in the shade. Or, grow windflowers mixed with perennials that stay dormant until late spring to early summer, such as astilbe or ferns. Avoid sites shaded in winter and early spring; that's where you'll get fewer flowers. In cooler climates, windflowers grow in full sun all year, but shelter from hot summer sun is advisable in the South. In frost-free and rare-frost areas, windflower does

WINDFLOWER

NAMED SELECTIONS

All windflower blossoms have bright yellow centers. When plants are tagged simply as *Anemone blanda*, the blossoms are usually blue to violet.

'BLUE SHADES': blue-violet
'CHARMER': rosy pink with inner ring of white
'INGRAMII': deep blue-violet
'PINK STAR': pale pink
'RADAR': purplish red
'VIOLET STAR': bright violet with inner ring of white
'WHITE SPLENDOUR': bright white

C

D

not come back reliably, making it an annual. Where winters are a little colder, windflower reappears each spring.

Fertile, woodsy soil is ideal, but windflower will adapt to just about any soil that drains well. Mix sand, gypsum, and chunky compost into heavy clay soils to improve drainage. Raised beds, slopes, and containers are also good spots for growing windflowers. Look for places where you'll see plants up close, else you may miss them. At the front of beds, sprinkled along paths and walkways, beside benches, and planting beds beside entries are good locations for including windflower.

Though it is easily forgotten until spring blooms appear, windflower requires forethought. It must be planted in autumn, just as daffodil bulbs must be. (This makes it easy to plant these two together.) In autumn, windflowers are sold as tubers. The day before planting, soak tubers over-night inside the house by placing them bumpy-side down in a shallow pan and covering with water. Prepare beds by turning over the soil to a depth of 12 inches; work amendments in well. Plant tubers bumpy-side up no deeper than 2.5 inches below the soil surface. (If there's not an obvious bumpy side, don't worry. Lay the tuber horizontally in the soil.) Water the bed of newly planted tubers and then leave it alone. Sprouts will appear in early spring, producing a small starter crop of blossoms. Flowering increases with age. Plants drop seeds, increasing windflower's spread in all but the hottest parts of the South. You'll get a larger, thicker carpet of

(C) Windflowers set seed and slowly spread to form carpets of spring color. Here, they grow before an evergreen background of leatherleaf mahonia.

(D) Though *Anemone blanda* plants are only 3 to 4 inches high, the flowers are a little bigger than what you may expect from such a low grower. Some blooms reach 2 inches across.

windflowers from dropped seed if the soil adjacent to existing plants is hospitable. This is why it is wise to prepare entire beds even when planting a mere handful of tubers. You can also grow windflowers from seed in the spring, though sprouts may not appear until autumn or even the following spring. Whether self-sown or grown from store-bought seed, windflower seedlings won't bloom until their second year.

Flowering on established plants can last for a month or more. Regular water, gently applied after flowering begins, helps keep the blossoms coming. However, roots must dry completely between waterings, so spring rains may prove sufficient. A short mound of finely cut foliage remains after spent flowers fade away. During summer the leaves fade away, too, so don't worry when they yellow and wither—and don't overwater windflowers in an attempt to freshen the foliage. Plants disappear entirely in hot weather, and they won't reemerge until the following spring. You may want to mark the location of your patch so you don't forget and dig it up later. Once windflowers are started, you really don't have to do anything but enjoy the blossoms every spring for years to come.

Annuals

SINGLE-SEASON BEDDING PLANTS

Caladium

Caladium x *hortulanum*

Also sold as *Caladium bicolor*

Caladiums and impatiens are the peanut butter and jelly of the Southern shade garden in summer. They're not unexpected but there's nothing wrong with relying on the classics. Large, colorful leaves renew the caladium's status as a traditional favorite when the weather heats up each year. Though potted plants are sometimes sold, most gardeners plant the tubers. Starting with a brown blob and ending up with a lush plant is a process that's economical and rewarding. Leaf stalks grow from eyes on tubers. The bigger the tuber, the more eyes it has and the more pretty leaves you'll get. That's why jumbo tubers cost the most. Never put caladium tubers in the refrigerator—the tubers must be kept warm and dry until they're planted.

Caladiums are tropicals and require warm soil. If the thermometer is still dropping below 65°F at night, it's too early to plant. Because climates vary, some lucky homeowners can plant their tubers earlier in the season than others—they'll get to enjoy the decorative foliage longer, too. In general, most Southern gardeners can get their tubers in the ground in mid-April, making tax day as good a guideline as any. Eager gardeners can start tubers early in pots indoors and transplant them later when nights are warm.

The nodding, painted leaves of caladiums add a refreshing quality to the shadows. Modest sunlight keeps leaf colors rich, but hot sun will keep you holding a hose all summer, so look for in-between areas. Sun-tolerant caladium selections help take away the fear of sun scorch, but direct rays of blazing western sun are usually best avoided. Morning sun is fine for all caladiums, particularly if that's when you water them.

GETTING ACQUAINTED

Annual bedding plant

6 to 30 inches high and wide, depending on selection

Large, heart-shaped leaves in white, red, pink, and many variations

Rapid rate of growth

Partial shade; most selections do best when sheltered from hot afternoon sun

Fertile, well-drained soil that's watered regularly; not for dry soil or consistently wet soil

Good choice for filling front layer of beds with color, growing in containers, near shaded patios, entries, benches, and ponds; plant within reach of sprinklers or hose

Pairs well with mondo grass, liriope, impatiens, astilbe, dead nettle, hydrangeas, camellia, bluestar, melampodium, wishbone flower, aucuba, hosta, Japanese painted fern, and other ferns

Zones 7–10

Grow caladiums for their decorative leaves. Plants produce flowers, which redirects energy from leaf production. If you like, you can cut the flower stalks near the ground to remove them and encourage more leaf growth.

A   B   C

(A) Beds of single colors, such as the 'June Bride' whites, make a big impact.
(B) Grow caladiums in containers by setting the pot in the shade and watering frequently. Don't forget to feed pot-grown caladiums.
(C) Cut caladium leaves are lovely in arrangements and last for weeks. Trim the stems again after removing them from the plant. Cut leaves set in water may wilt the first day, but this is normal and they soon rehydrate.

SQUIRRELING AWAY TUBERS

You can dig caladium tubers in autumn to store through the winter but second-year leaves rarely match the first year's show. Wait until foliage has withered to dig tubers. Rinse them, allow them to dry completely, and store in old pantyhose knotted to keep each tuber separate. Hang them in a warm place that isn't humid, and inspect for signs of fungus or rot before replanting in spring. You may want to mix old tubers in with new ones of the same selection. This way, your expenditure will be reduced but you won't have to rely completely on old tubers for summer color. Or, consider caladiums annuals and start over again each spring. To get the freshest tubers, order them ahead of time directly from growers. Shipping will be delayed until the appropriate planting time in your area. Tubers, properly called corms, are starchy inside like a potato, not layered like a bulb.

Grow caladiums in containers or prepared beds, not mere holes chiseled into hard soil. It takes some effort to turn over soil to make it soft and fluffy. Fortunately, caladiums look best when grown in a thick patch, so a small bed is actually more dramatic than a big, long row. If your soil is sandy, mix in equal parts peat moss and composted bark to enrich it and improve water retention. If your soil is heavy clay, add equal parts bark nuggets, sand, and peat moss. This will aid drainage, an important aspect of growing caladiums. The tubers need moisture, but they'll rot if they're constantly wet. Never add manure to caladium beds.

Set the tubers anywhere from 8 to 15 inches apart. The knobby side of the tuber is the topside. It may have squiggly brown roots attached—these should point up, not down. The smooth, hairless side is the bottom of the tuber. It you can't tell which is which, don't worry because the plant will figure it out, though it may take longer for shoots to emerge if you plant tubers upside-down. Cover tubers with 2 to 3 inches of soil—no more and no less. Gently soak the bed with a hose after planting and repeat once a week until shoots appear. After leaf stalks are actively growing, you can water more often to speed growth. As long as the soil drains well, you can water every few days or even daily during heat waves. Caladiums that collapse from thirst can be saved with prompt application of water but such plants will never quite regain their previous vigor. So if you're going on vacation and figuring out who'll feed the cat, remember to include how to keep caladiums watered in the plans. However, frequent watering does leach nutrients from the soil, making it a good idea to feed caladiums every six weeks with a balanced fertilizer such as 6–6–6 or 8–8–8. Follow label directions, and don't apply too much.

Impatiens

I mpatiens have the same growing requirements as caladiums. But while caladiums are beloved for their foliage, impatiens are famous for their flowers. Growing impatiens isn't difficult if you get the conditions right and don't mind watering. Content impatiens bloom their heads off and produce numerous offspring from seed.

It's critical to avoid planting impatiens where hot afternoon rays will beat down on plants. Morning sunlight is usually fine, but if impatiens gets too many hours of direct rays, they'll wilt, even in the morning. Dappled shade is best. All-day shade can make impatiens grow tall and thin with few flowers.

Don't plant impatiens beyond reach of a hose or sprinkler system. These summer flowers love water. Watch for signs of wilting—drooping leaves are a dead giveaway that impatiens are thirsty. Fortunately, wilted impatiens revive quickly after a good soaking. Always water in the morning so plants won't remain wet after sundown, which leads to fungal problems.

Provide impatiens with fertile soil that drains well. Amend soil as you would for caladiums. Though most annuals are usually so pumped up on fertilizer by the time they leave the nursery that they don't require any at more at planting time, it is a good idea to add some slow-release fertilizer beneath the roots of each impatiens plant. The high water needs of this annual tend to leave soil impoverished, so tucking in a snack for later will help combat this problem.

Leggy impatiens can be pinched back. Removing a section of each too-long stem will make plants bushy. Not only does this encourage a nice, rounded plant shape, but it also prompts flowering. Though it is hard to bring yourself to do it, removing as much as half of the growth of young impatiens upon planting will yield fuller plants and numerous blossoms. When shopping, choose impatiens that have just enough open flowers to make sure you're getting the color you want. But remember, it is better

GETTING ACQUAINTED

Annual bedding plant

8 to 12 inches high and wide

Flat or double flowers cover plants for months during warm weather

May self-seed

Rapid growth rate

Mostly shady

Fertile, well-drained soil that's watered regularly; not for dry soil or consistently wet soil

Good choice for filling front layer of beds with color, growing in containers, near shaded entries and patios; plant within reach of sprinklers or hose

Pairs well with mondo grass, astilbe, caladium, dead nettle, wishbone flower, hydrangeas, bluestar, hosta, variegated bigleaf periwinkle, Japanese painted fern, and various ferns

Zones 7–10

Impatiens bloom beautifully in spots that are mostly shady. Regular water is required, but impatiens that have collapsed from thirst can usually be saved with some quick hydration therapy—a good drenching with a hose.

(A)

(B)

C

D

(A) Double-flowering impatiens resemble little roses.

(B) Impatiens thrive in shaded containers with regular water. These double-flowering impatiens are mixed with feathery plumes of asparagus fern and 'White Nancy' dead nettle.

(C) Impatiens are eye-catching when planted in swaths of color. Here, impatiens is edged with ageratum.

(D) Solid white impatiens make a sophisticated choice for the formal gardens of the Biedenharn Foundation, Monroe, Louisiana

to buy buds than open blossoms, so pass up taller, more colorful plants in favor of squatty ones that will bloom after you get them home.

Single-color plantings of impatiens are always attractive. With so many bright choices, it is hard to be content with just one or two. But multiple color mixtures can quickly become garish. If mixing two colors is what you want, look for hues that are just a step or two apart. Pale pink and medium pink will blend better than hot pink and strong orange planted together. The loud colors are better off by themselves. To mix colors, grow the two hues in random placement together in the bed or container. Alternating impatiens to produce noticeably striped beds can ruin the beauty of a shade garden quicker than a dead possum on the front lawn.

Melampodium

Melampodium paludosum

Also sold as butter daisy, gold medallion flower, star daisy
Not to be confused with Blackfoot daisy (*Melampodium leucanthemum*), which has white flowers

Keeping shade-loving plants happy can become tiresome. They want shade but they want a little sun, too—but not too much sun and not at the wrong time of day. Sometimes you simply need a plant that will bloom in shadowy spots but doesn't have to go into hiding during hot summer afternoons. Meet melampodium.

Melampodium is often listed as an annual for full sun. When it is watered with fair regularity, it thrives in all-day sun. Northern gardeners rely on full sun to generate enough heat to coax this plant into bloom. Because that's not an issue in the South, we can grow melampodium in partial shade and enjoy just as many golden flowers. This is one plant that doesn't reduce its efforts when sunlight is reduced, and it can take the glare of any direct rays that come its way. As any Southern gardener knows, that's a valuable combination.

This daisy-faced annual bedding plant blooms heavily from spring to the first frost. The golden flowers nestle against a mound of bright green leaves. Though the blooms are just about 1 inch across, there are enough of them to make quite a show. There's no need to remove spent blossoms, so don't waste your time deadheading. This plant drops faded flowers discreetly and immediately makes more. Expect nearly nonstop color.

Grow melampodium in average to fertile soil. Moistened roots promote growth and melampodium will appreciate regular water. But too dry is better than too wet for this plant—soil must drain well. When given some shade, it will become quite drought tolerant for an annual. Don't plant melampodium in all-day shade or damp soil. Clay soil should be amended

GETTING ACQUAINTED

Annual bedding plant

8 to 36 inches high and wide, depending on selection

Golden, daisy-faced flowers framed by green foliage

Rapid growth rate

Resistant to insects and disease

Partial shade to full sun; not for all-day shade

Average soil; not for wet soil

Average to low water, quite drought tolerant when grown in partial shade

Good choice for planting beside steps, patios, low decks, swimming pools, mailboxes, in containers, planters, or beds

Pairs well with aucuba, mondo grass, Japanese painted fern, rhododendron, Lenten rose, caladium, climbing and shrub hydrangeas, Virginia sweetspire, bluestar, and hosta

Zones 7–10

You don't have to pinch off spent blossoms to keep the flowers coming. Melampodium blooms for months without ceasing.

Melampodium has no qualms about growing in the sun but it will bloom equally well in partial shade. That means it is tough enough to withstand any hot afternoon rays that might reach it in the summer. Here melampodium grows with blue salvia and ageratum.

with organic matter to improve drainage (or replaced with a raised bed of friable soil). Once you've got it going, melampodium will brighten your garden for months. If left in beds until damaged by frost, plants may reseed and show up voluntarily the following spring. Melampodium is a good choice for growing in containers, too.

NAMED SELECTIONS

'MILLION GOLD': 8 to 10 inches high and wide, produces few seeds

'MELANIE' AND 'DERBY': 10 inches high and wide

'LEMON DELIGHT': 12 inches high and wide with light yellow flowers

'SHOWSTAR': 14 to 24 inches high and wide, heavy seed producer

'MEDALLION': 24 to 36 inches high and wide

Wishbone Flower

Seasonal color that thrives in humid heat and blooms in the shade? It's not just wishful thinking. Wishbone flower is a tropical plant that's useful as a warm-weather annual. You can buy seeds to start in flats indoors in late winter or wait until spring and purchase plants. With regular water and pinching back to promote fresh growth, wishbone flower will bloom until the first frost. After that, you can bring yours inside to pamper as a houseplant in a sunny window through the winter or you can let it go to that great compost heap in the sky along with the rest of your fair-weather flowers. When grown in moist soil in frost-free climates, wishbone flower spreads to form a self-seeding groundcover.

The velvety blossoms of wishbone are often compared to snapdragons. If you look down the flowers' yellow throats, you'll see the pair of stamens that gives this plant its name. Flower colors range from shades of blue, purple, and pink to nearly black. Plants grow to form rounded clumps of foliage decorated with blossoms. Even though blooms are profuse, wishbone flower is a plant that's better seen up close and personal. The rich, pansy-soft petals can't be properly appreciated from afar, and the colors don't carry across the landscape the way impatiens' do. Grow wishbone flowers in containers so you can arrange them for optimum viewing and move them away from direct sun. This annual is also an excellent choice for hanging baskets, window boxes, and planters in the shade. Though it doesn't exactly trail, the flowers and foliage do cascade somewhat, making wishbone flower good for the front row in a mixed container. Wishbone flower will also thrive in flowerbeds in the right setting, but you'll enjoy the luscious flowers more if they're grown closer to your eyes than to your feet.

GETTING ACQUAINTED

Annual bedding plant

8 to 12 inches high and wide; rounded

Velvety warm-season blooms in shades of purple, blue, pink, and nearly black

All-day shade to dappled shade; avoid hot direct rays and dry soil

Moist, fertile soil is best; amend soil with compost and peat prior to planting; water retention products may be added to soil in scant quantities for hanging baskets and container-grown plants; requires frequent watering

Good choice for pots, window boxes, hanging baskets, planters, and raised beds; best seen up close

Pairs well with variegated bigleaf periwinkle, mondo grass, impatiens, astilbe, Japanese painted fern, caladium, and other shade-loving annuals

Zones 7–10

Wishbone flower makes a rounded ball of flowers that's ideal for containers and hanging baskets in shady spots.

A

B

BEDDING PLANTS: ANNUALS

PINCH AN INCH

Keep the flowers coming by pinching back the stems of wishbone flower to encourage new growth. To jumpstart blooming during a lull, clip the plant back gently in an all-over haircut. Removing spent blossoms doesn't promote flowering the way pinching does because the plant needs to grow more stem to set buds; removing ends of stems promotes fresh growth. That's why the wishbone flower grows in a nice round ball—the stems are growing in all directions. If you let the flowers go to seed, you can collect the tiny seeds from green pods for next year.

NAMED SELECTIONS

SUMMER WAVE® SERIES: various colors; plants exhibit even better heat tolerance
CATALINA® SERIES: various colors; plant form is more cascading

Wishbone flower isn't one of those plant-em-and-forget-em annuals. You'll need to fuss over it some. If that's not appealing, consider buying just a couple of small plants to see how compatible the two of you are. (Those big, lush hanging baskets are tempting, but make sure you're committed to watering before surrendering to botanical desire.) You'll need to give wishbone flower a drink of water every day unless it rains. For plants grown under the shelter of porches, rain doesn't let you off the hook. Plants set in rich potting mix in the shade may be able to skip two days of watering, three max. Don't drown your plants in an attempt to water less frequently—it really is necessary to commit to watering regularly to keep roots moist but not consistently wet. Mulch can help preserve soaked-in soil moisture.

Shade is essential for growing wishbone flower. Plants will bloom in all-day shade or partial shade. Dappled shade is fine, but make sure hot afternoon rays don't reach these plants. Morning sun is not as lethal but if it's direct and hot, then it should be avoided, too. Flower colors fade and plants decline and die when grown in too much sun. Your best bet is to place wishbone flower in those dark spots where you always wish you had more sunlight.

C

(A) Tuck wishbone flower in compositions of other plants that take shade, such as impatiens and polka-dot plant, *Hypoestes sanguinolenta*, shown here.

(B) Removing spent flowers doesn't keep wishbone flower in bloom, but pinching back tips of foliage does.

(C) For pink and white flowers marked with yellow, look for a wishbone flower tagged 'Clown Rose Improved'.

Shrubs

Showy Shrubs

Annabelle Hydrangea

Hydrangea arborescens
'Annabelle'

Shrubs: Showy

Whoever Annabelle is, she must be mighty flattered to have such a lovely plant named after her. 'Annabelle' is a superior selection of the native smooth hydrangea, *Hydrangea arborescens*. Large, creamy pom-pom blossoms brighten garden shadows in early to midsummer. As if this show weren't enough, Annabelle hydrangea offers interesting stages of flowering. Blooms first appear in late spring or early summer as large, tightly packed balls of clear green petals. The limey color gives way to brilliant white and blooms stay that way for weeks. Then, the flowers fade again to a dull green by summer's end and turn tan in autumn. The flower balls shrink as they dry on the stems, persisting through the winter as oatmeal-colored bundles decorating bare branch tips.

Like other hydrangeas, the selection 'Annabelle' dislikes long hours of hot, direct sun, so plant yours in partial shade. Choose a spot that's protected from western afternoon summer sun, although a bit of morning sun is good for flowering. Avoid dense, all-day shade. The farther south you live, the more shade and water your Annabelle hydrangeas will require. Make sure to choose locations where at least a few hours of filtered sunlight can reach plants.

All hydrangeas like water, and Annabelle is no exception. Water regularly during the growing season, particularly when the weather is hot and dry. Plants wilt when they're too dry or receiving too much direct sun. Water wilted plants immediately to revive them. Annabelles don't require automatic sprinkler systems, but they do thrive when grown in landscapes that have them. Soaker hoses are a good idea, too. These pretty shrubs can't compete with the roots of mature trees for water, so you'll need to build a raised bed with its own watering system in such a setting.

GETTING ACQUAINTED

Deciduous shrub (bare in winter)

3 to 4 feet high by 3 to 5 feet wide

Flower balls grow up to 12 inches across and change hues from green to white to green again

Moderate to rapid rate of growth

Insect and disease resistant

Partial shade

Fertile soil that's moist but well drained; slightly acidic soil is best

Good choice for planting as masses in lightly shaded beds beside patios or in the open landscape, growing beside low walls or behind beds of perennials that fade by late summer, and tucked into foundation planting for seasonal color near evergreen plants

Pairs well with camellia, astilbe, hosta, Japanese painted fern, Japanese kerria, caladium, bleeding heart, periwinkle, cardinal flower, foamflower, Lenten rose, Solomon's seal, celandine poppy, star magnolia, bluebells, Pinxterbloom azalea, red buckeye, melampodium, French hydrangea, and dead nettle; grow in front of eastern hemlock

Zones 3–9

Annabelle hydrangeas need to be watered, but an abundance of large blossoms make it worthwhile.

A

B

C

D

(A) Blossoms start off as limey green balls that fade to cream.

(B) By midsummer, the large puffballs have turned snowy white.

(C) Blossoms regress to light green at summer's end.

(D) The spent blooms of Annabelle hydrangea dry tan and persist on stalks through winter.

DRYING FLOWERS

The blossoms of Annabelle hydrangeas are easy to dry for use in arrangements. Clip faded blooms on 6-inch stems in autumn. Bundle blooms by their stems with rubber bands and hang upside down in a cool, dry place for a few weeks. The resulting dried flowers keep their ball shape. Though the tan color may sound unappealing, dried hydrangea blossoms taken on an almost golden hue when used in arrangements or wreaths beside dark green foliage such as holly, magnolia, or Christmas tree trimmings. The dried flowers also combine well with sprays of nandina berries, dried seedheads from purple coneflowers, okra seedpods, and the cones of hemlocks or pines.

Watering is less critical in cooler regions, such as upper elevations, though drought conditions mean that everyone must water their Annabelle hydrangeas.

It is well worth a little effort to grow this lovely plant. Amending the soil at planting time makes things easier later on. Mix humus-rich compost and native soil in even amounts; don't leave out the organic matter. If your soil is heavy clay, you'll need to build a raised bed to improve drainage to keep your Annabelles happy. Mulch newly planted shrubs and soak roots with a trickling hose.

Plan to fertilize and prune Annabelles most years, although it's okay to miss a year or two. In late winter, feed leafless shrubs with a balanced fertilizer such as 10–10–10 to promote vigorous growth. Late winter is also the correct time to cut branches back to within a foot of the ground to encourage flowering. Unlike many hydrangeas that boom on stems produced the year before, Annabelle hydrangeas bloom on new wood, so there's no concern about cutting off buds grown last year.

Annabelle hydrangeas have few enemies besides drought, so watering is the only remaining task. Your efforts will be rewarded with pretty green shrubs that produce plenty of big snowballs of blossoms. A fertilized, watered Annabelle hydrangea can produce multiple flower clusters as large as 10 to 12 inches in diameter. Grow single plant as an accent or set multiple shrubs where they can grow together as a mass. As the blossoms of your Annabelle hydrangeas progress from light green to white, back to green again, and on to winter tan, you'll find plenty to admire.

Beautyberry

Callicarpa americana

Also sold as American beautyberry, French mulberry

Shrubs: Showy

Beautyberry is a big, ungainly shrub with two redeeming qualities. First, it grows almost anywhere, including that troublesome setting near large trees known as dry shade. Second, it produces vivid, eye-catching, head-turning, what-is-that purple berries in autumn. Leaves are still on the plant when the slightly arching stalks become ringed with clusters of bright, shiny berries. But the foliage soon withers and drops, revealing the crop of color more clearly. The fruit persists into winter, eventually shriveling and drying into dark little inoffensive raisins—that is, if birds haven't cleaned out the berries first. The purple fruit attracts many wild birds, most notably mockingbirds.

Beautyberry is outstanding in the autumn landscape, a nice surprise among the traditional reds and yellows of the season. Cut branches laden with berries are excellent for use in arrangements. Fortunately, this shrub flowers on new growth, so you can cut plenty of branches for use in decorating without removing next year's berries. In early spring, you can also severely prune an overgrown or woody plant that's producing less fruit to induce new growth and better berry loads. Beautyberries growing in upper parts of the South may suffer freeze damage during cold winters; such shrubs can also be cut nearly to the ground in spring to prompt new growth. Plants that have been whacked back early in the growing season can usually be counted on to produce berries the following autumn, though the shrubs themselves will naturally be smaller in size for a few years.

The durability of this native plant is legendary. You can grow beautyberry in the woods, at a beach house, or pretty much anywhere in your landscape where you've got room. Beautyberry can grow in full sun, where it will produce gobs of berries, but it is particularly useful for par-

GETTING ACQUAINTED

Deciduous shrub (bare in winter)

4 to 8 feet high by 4 to 6 feet wide

Eye-catching purple berries appear in clusters around stems in autumn

Moderate to rapid rate of growth

Tolerates heat, drought, and sandy soil

May be invasive in frost-free areas due to birds spreading seeds

Native

Partial shade to full sun

Any kind of soil that's not extremely alkaline or heavy clay

Good choice for dry shade, natural areas, coastal landscapes and beach houses, cutting gardens, autumn perennial beds, native plant collections, dressing up the edges of woods, and attracting wild birds

Pairs well with mondo grass, Spanish bluebell, eastern hemlock, yellow archangel, star magnolia, leatherleaf, mahonia, dead nettle, fothergilla, oakleaf hydrangea, rhododendron, Virginia sweetspire, redbud, and tall pines

Zones 6–10

If you enjoy wild birds, plant a beautyberry where you can see it from a window, patio, or porch. Many species of birds feast on the berries from autumn into winter.

A

B

C

tially shaded areas. Because established shrubs tolerate dry conditions, beautyberry is a good choice for growing beneath large trees with wide spreading roots. Such trees tend to consume most of the available moisture, making it difficult for other plants to grow, but beautyberry rises to the challenge. This shrub can even grow in dense shade, but branches will be sparse and berry production will be reduced. Though flowering is inconspicuous, the pale summer blossoms hidden by big yellow-green leaves are essential to berry production.

Any soil that's not extremely alkaline or heavy clay is suitable for growing beautyberry. Soil that's wet, dry, fertile, poor, or even sandy will do. Mulch shrubs with pine straw to lower the soil pH and mimic natural conditions of the piney woodlands where beautyberries grow wild. Make sure you've got room for a plant that's going to get big: A 6-foot high and wide beautyberry is not uncommon. Plants are irregular in shape, with stiff branches that arch at the ends. The form is open and loose and somewhat awkward. Though its shape keeps it out of most formal gardens, a single beautyberry is actually a perfect foil for a frame of dense, dark green boxwoods or hollies. Fences and walls make good backgrounds for beautyberries, too. You may have to find a native plant sale to purchase beautyberry, as it is not commonly sold at landscape centers.

(A) Late in the season, beautyberry fruit begins to dry on the branches. The brilliant purple color lasts for months before finally fading to shriveled black.
(B) Cut branches of purple berries are prized by florists for use in arrangements.
(C) *Callicarpa americana* var. *lactea* has white fruit. Though initially attractive, the fruit browns as it ages. This isn't a problem of the native purple-berried species.

Fothergilla

Fothergilla is a double feature in the landscape. With two seasons of show, this easy-to-grow shrub has plenty to offer. Spring brings green leaves and bushy white flowers that are often compared to bottlebrushes. The lightly scented blossoms stand up like fluffy candles. After spending the summer unobtrusively cloaked in dark green leathery leaves, fothergilla takes the stage again in autumn. As the season changes, the foliage assumes a painted appearance, turning hues of orange, scarlet, and gold. Autumn color is quite reliable and doesn't appear to be dependent on many environmental factors, though sunlight is necessary for bright tones. That's why its best to plant fothergilla in the front of a shady bed, where it will receive sun for about half a day or filtered sunlight for much of the day. Homeowners in cooler parts of the South, including mountain areas, can plant fothergilla in all-day sun if they're willing to water. However, shrubs grown in most parts of the region require partial shade to thrive.

Fothergilla is a low-maintenance plant. Pruning is not necessary. It does require acidic soil and performs poorly in high pH soils, which is common in areas with a lot of limestone. Fertile soil that's moist but not consistently wet is best, but fothergilla is an adaptable sort and will grow in dry or wet soil, too. Occasional flooding is no problem for this shrub. Fothergilla grown in moist soil may form colonies of new plants by sending up shoots from the roots, a habit known as suckering. This is not a problem if you've got space to fill.

Once you've gotten young plants through their first hot season, you can pretty much forget about them. Fothergilla grows slowly, filling in the available space. Young plants are upright in form but become broader and

---

Fothergilla major

Also sold as large fothergilla, witch-alder, mountain witch-alder, *Fothergilla monticola*

GETTING ACQUAINTED

Deciduous shrub (bare in winter)

4 to 8 feet high by 2 to 4 feet wide

Creamy, bottlebrush-like flowers borne in spring; reliably bright autumn color

Slow rate of growth

Insect and disease resistant

Partial shade to full sun

Acidic well-drained soil; rich and moist is best, but plants will tolerate dry soil; not for alkaline soil

Good choice for shady beds, natural areas, growing along the edges of woodlands or ponds, and tucked into foundation planting beside evergreen plants

Pairs well with eastern hemlock, astilbe, aucuba, windflower, star magnolia, smilax, yellow archangel, beautyberry, Japanese kerria, pieris, camellia, celandine poppy, holly fern, leatherleaf mahonia, mondo grass, rhododendron, Pinxterbloom azalea, Solomon's seal, dead nettle, Virginia sweetspire, gooseneck loosestrife, bluestar, cardinal flower, red buckeye, and foamflower

Zones 5–9

Fothergilla brightens shadowy beds in spring with creamy flowers.

more rounded as they age and as space permits. If planted in a crowded situation, fothergilla will adapt and grow an irregular form, like something found in the woods. This naturalistic look is attractive but may not be suitable for formal landscapes.

Fothergilla is native across a swath of the Southeast, but unfortunately it is not as readily available in the retail trade as it should be. You may have to seek native plant sales or specialty nurseries to find it for sale, but fothergilla is worth the hunt. You'll love it planted in front of shade-loving evergreens, such as eastern hemlock, rhododendron, or pieris. The year-round foliage of such plants makes a perfect background for showcasing fothergilla's delicate spring flowers and glowing autumn colors.

(A) The fuzzy flowers of fothergilla are lightly honey-scented.
(B) Fothergilla shrubs that receive some sunlight turn bright colors in autumn.

NAMED SELECTIONS

'ARKANSAS BEAUTY': slightly more compact, 6 feet high and wide, plenty of blossoms

'MT. AIRY': known for its autumn color

BLUE MIST® AND BLUE SHADOW®: leaves are bluish green in spring and autumn

'GARDENII': dwarf selection, grows more slowly and stays compact longer; may eventually grow 5 feet high.

French Hydrangea

When you say hydrangea, this is the plant most people will think of. Sporting summertime ball-shaped blossoms of pink, blue, white, or sometimes even purple, French hydrangeas are old-time shade gardening favorites. These flowering shrubs are also known as common or bigleaf hydrangeas mopheads. Whatever you call it, you'll love this plant for its showy flowers. The blooms are big and long lasting. Blossoms also retain their color fairly well when cut and dried for later use in arrangements.

Pink and blue are French hydrangea's most common colors. Though there are named varieties that produce specific hues, the blossom color of most unnamed French hydrangeas is dependent upon the pH of the soil in which the plant is growing. French hydrangeas planted in areas with high soil pH, or alkaline soils, produce pink blossoms. Plants grown in areas with naturally low soil pH, or acidic soils, produce blue blossoms. Human nature being what it is, we all want the opposite color of whatever naturally occurs in our landscape. If you like, you can be different from your neighbors by chemically reversing the color process. Add lime to acidic soils to produce pink flowers or apply aluminum sulfate to pink-flowering plants to turn their blossoms blue (see page 70). Or, you can be lazy like me and take what you get and learn to like it.

Hydrangeas prefer to be well hydrated—hence the name—so plant yours where you can keep the soil reasonably moist. Don't plant hydrangeas beyond reach of a hose or sprinkler system unless you particularly enjoy toting heavy watering cans. Don't think that always-wet soil is the answer, either—standing water in planting holes will cause roots to rot. Moist soil that drains well is ideal. In much of the South, moist soil

GETTING ACQUAINTED

Deciduous shrub (bare in winter)

4 to 5 feet high by 4 to 5 feet wide

Large, showy round flowers come in pink, blue, white, or occasionally purple; blooms in summer

Moderate to slow rate of growth

Filtered shade; protect from hot afternoon sun

Moist soil that isn't consistently wet; fertile soil promotes best growth

Good choice for shady beds visible from outdoor seating areas, tucked into foundation plantings, grown at entries, in front of evergreen plants, walls, and fences

Pairs well with astilbe, Japanese painted fern, cardinal flower, caladium, melampodium, Japanese kerria, Solomon's seal, trillium, bleeding heart, hosta, Lenten rose, red buckeye, mondo grass, periwinkle, foamflower, dead nettle, celandine poppy, star magnolia, Annabelle hydrangea, Pinxterbloom azalea, and ferns. Grow in front of eastern hemlock, camellia, or rhododendron

Zones 6–9

Few shade plants are as beloved as the French hydrangea. It's like growing clouds on a shrub.

NAMED SELECTIONS

'NIKKO BLUE': 4 to 6 feet tall; deep blue flowers when grown in acidic soil; may be purplish in alkaline soil

'ELF': Sometimes sold as Pink Elf®; 2 to 3 feet tall; pink flowers in any soil, though they may have a purplish hue when grown in acidic soil

'FOREVER PINK': 2 to 3 feet tall; flowers normally pink, but may require dolomitic lime to keep color true when grown in acidic soil

ENDLESS SUMMER®: Blooms nearly nonstop from June until frost. Light pink or light blue flowers, depending on soil pH. Unlike other French hydrangeas, Endless Summer® blooms on new wood, so removing spent blossoms throughout the growing season will encourage fresh flowering, though doing so is optional. Also known as *Hydrangea* 'Bailmer', this plants is cold hardy as far north as zone 4.

BLUSHING BRIDE®: Large white balls of flowers appear all summer long. Bred in Georgia by Dr. Michael Dirr using Endless Summer® as the parent plant, this plants is cold tolerant to zone 5.

MESSING WITH COLOR

The blossom color of *Hydrangea macrophylla* is dependent upon the pH of the soil in which plants are grown. You can change the pH to change the flower color.

Acidic soil turns blossoms blue; some named selections are bred to flower blue in most soil.

Alkaline soil produces pink flowers. You can buy named selections that are reliably pink in most soil, too.

For pink flowers, add dolomitic lime several times a year. Overdoing it with lime may cause an iron deficiency; if leaves turn yellow, stop liming. Or, add a handful of granular Espoma Bulb-Tone® to the planting hole and sprinkle some beneath plants twice a year, in winter and early spring. Also apply fertilizers with high levels of phosphorus such as 10–25–10. Phosphorus helps to prevent aluminum from being taken up in the plant's system, so flowers remain pink.

Concrete paving and concrete wall footings leach lime into the soil, resulting in pink blooms. If a hydrangea bred to produce exclusively blue flowers is planted near a foundation or sidewalk, flowers may wind up an attractive purple shade.

Low soil pH produces blue flowers. To turn pink flowers blue, apply a soil acidifier, such as Espoma Holly-Tone® 4–6–4. Follow manufacturer's recommendations for rates and apply in spring and autumn. Rake away mulch, sprinkle on the soil beneath the shrub, cover with mulch again, and water. Miracid® is another product that helps keep soil around plants acidic for blue blossoms. Avoid fertilizers high in phosphorus. Adding aluminum sulfate will also yield blue flowers.

A

B

is hard to come by during hot summertime, so you may have to settle for well-drained soil and a handy hose. Add plenty of organic matter at planting and plan to water frequently during dry spells.

French hydrangeas are shade-loving shrubs, but a little sun is necessary for prolific flowering. A dose of morning sun will do; be aware that the hot afternoon sun of Southern summers will reduce hydrangeas to horticultural stir-fry. Sites with all-day filtered shade or a few hours of morning sun are best. Water wilted plants quickly to reverse drying affects of hot, direct sun; relocating plants to a more hospitable

C

D

E

F

spot is the best long-term solution for frequent wilting or crisp, browned leaves. The farther south you live, the more intense the sun is, and the more hours of daily shade French hydrangeas require.

Pruning is occasionally needed to keep plants bushy or to control size. Unless you're willing to sacrifice flowers, the only time you should ever prune a French hydrangea is immediately after blooming ceases. If you wait until later, you'll cut off the buds for next year's flowers. That's because most French hydrangeas are known as old wood bloomers, meaning their blossoms form on the previous year's growth. If you prune at the wrong time, you'll forgo a season of flowers, but the plant will bloom the following year as long as you don't continue to cut.

Winter reduces these shrubs to clusters of barren sticks. To keep winter beds from becoming boring, it is a good idea to position hydrangeas near other plants that have evergreen leaves or interesting berries during the cold months. French hydrangeas can tolerate cold winters, but occasionally a badly timed cold snap or severe winter may kill all or most of a plant's branches back to the ground. Younger plants are more susceptible to winter damage than well-established ones. But most French hydrangeas recover remarkably well, sending out vigorous new shoots in the spring.

If a cold snap zaps your hydrangeas, wait until new shoots appear before cutting off any branches killed by low temperatures. If you remove dead branches too soon, you may encourage new growth too early in the season. It is always a good idea to gently scratch the bark with your thumbnail for signs of green before pruning—the branches you think are dead may merely be dormant. If you see green beneath the bark, leave the branches on the plant and let nature take its course. You may temporarily experience reduced flowering on freeze-damaged plants, but French hydrangeas left alone will usually rebound just fine and return to their normal heavy-flower-producing habits the following summer.

(A) Modest amounts of lime added to acidic soil can result in purplish flowers. The selection 'Royal Purple' reliably blooms purple.

(B) A single French hydrangea makes an excellent specimen plant to add an accent to your landscape. Or, grow a quantity of these shrubs together in a blended mass.

(C) Keep hydrangeas happy by mulching roots to keep them moist in summer and warm in winter.

(D) When cut and dried, French hydrangea flowers fade in intensity but retain some of their original hue for years.

(E) When leaves droop, it is past time to water so get the hose out immediately. Hydrangeas perk up quickly after watering.

(F) When left on stalks, flowerheads turn tan in winter and last until replacements appear in spring.

Kerria japonica

Also sold as kerria

Japanese Kerria

GETTING ACQUAINTED

Deciduous shrub (bare in winter)

3 to 4 feet high by 5 to 6 feet wide; suckering habit causes clumps to widen with age

Golden yellow blooms cover plants in spring

Rapid rate of growth

Resistant to insects and disease

Drought tolerant

All-day or half-day's shade

Any soil except wet

Good choice for growing beneath deciduous trees, dry shade, on slopes, behind retaining walls, in natural areas, large beds, and areas hard to reach with a hose; not for formal, clipped gardens, and unsuitable for homeowners who want to shear things

Pairs well with oak trees, daffodil, bluestar, Spanish bluebell, smilax, climbing hydrangea, star magnolia, fothergilla, dead nettle, yellow archangel, hosta, gooseneck loosestrife, periwinkle, redbud, and hydrangeas; shows off nicely with a backdrop of eastern hemlock, pieris, camellia, rhododendron, or aucuba

Zones 4–9

Single-flowering Japanese kerria is a shrub that ought to be planted in more gardens. Big golden blooms brighten the shade with carefree color each spring.

It was one of those moments of truth that all landscape architects must face at some time or another. My neighbor had a gift certificate from a local nursery and wanted me to suggest a shrub to grow in the shade, but *not* a hydrangea. He wanted something different. Could I come up with a satisfactory recommendation off the top of my head? Japanese kerria sprang to mind, allowing me to maintain my professional dignity. Whew.

My neighbor was so pleased with this shrub he went back and bought a few more. And now that his Japanese kerria is producing suckers, he's

even invited me to dig up a few baby plants for my garden. Funny how that worked out. Ulterior motives aside, Japanese kerria is truly a great shrub for shade.

In springtime, flat golden flowers cover the plants known as single-flowering Japanese kerria, such as the named selection 'Shannon'. These plants grow as clumping shrubs. The prolific five-petaled flowers open after leaves have appeared. Because the blossoms are yellow, you'll find that many people assume its forsythia. But forsythia blooms best in full sun, not shade, and its flowers resemble shaggy confetti on leafless stems.

Kerria is deciduous, so it loses its leaves in autumn after they turn a lemony shade of yellow. Shrubs are bare in winter, although the major stems remain green. New shoots sprout from creeping roots each year, enlarging plants as they age. You can leave these suckers alone and let the shrubs grow denser and wider, or you can dig a few shoots here and there to start new plants elsewhere in your landscape. Cool, wet weather is the optimum time for transplanting.

A little sun is needed to encourage Japanese kerria to flower well. But because blooming occurs in spring before most hardwoods unfurl their leaves, you can plant these shrubs in areas that are deeply shaded by

A

B

C

D

E

(A) The simple flowers of single-flowering Japanese kerria look like something a child would draw. New leaves set off the golden blooms.

(B) As a shrub for shade, Japanese kerria is a less common alternative to hydrangeas or azaleas. Kerrias are green and fluffy in summer.

(C) The foliage of Japanese kerria turns lemony yellow in autumn before dropping for winter.

(D) Main stems remain green even after leaves yellow and drop.

(E) The spreading roots of Japanese kerria produce suckers, leafy sprouts that make new plants. You can chop the roots apart and move suckers or leave them alone to let your shrubs grow into larger clumps.

DOUBLE-FLOWERING JAPANESE KERRIA

Kerria japonica 'Pleniflora'

Double-flowering Japanese kerria are sprawling plants with rounded, ruffled flowers.

Like its single-flowering relative, the yellow blossoms of double-flowering Japanese kerria show up after foliage has appeared each spring. But there the resemblance ends. Each perfect little golden flower of 'Pleniflora' is a rounded puffball of tightly packed petals. This selection of Japanese kerria looks more like a sprawling rose than a shrub. It sends out long, arching sprays. This rustic habit of growth is far from neat and tidy, making double-flowering Japanese kerria best grown where it can lean on a split rail fence, tumble over a retaining wall, or decorate a blank wall. Keep pruning to a minimum. Remove dead branches, but allow the plant to sprawl at will (up to 12 feet). You'll be rewarded with a springtime show of ruffled golden pom-poms year after year.

EASY TO GROW

Both single- and double-flowering Japanese kerria thrive in moist, loamy soil, but these tough plants will adapt to less-than-perfect conditions without complaint. Newly planted kerria may require supplemental watering through a dry spring or during the plants' first encounters with hot weather. Established plants are tough and drought tolerant. They even thrive within the root zones of trees, a difficult spot for many shrubs because the tree roots get most of the moisture. Fertilizing Japanese kerria isn't necessary and can actually lead to reduced flowering, giving you an excellent excuse to skip that chore.

You can grow Japanese kerria beneath large shade trees that lose their leaves in winter. Because these shrubs bloom in spring when tree branches are still bare, adequate sunlight can reach the plants to promote flowering.

deciduous trees during summer. Kerria grows well beneath large oak trees, where decaying leaves improve the soil. Choose a location where you don't want a formally pruned, geometrically shaped shrub. Japanese kerria's habit is loose, airy, and open, and you really shouldn't try to prune it into an unnatural shape. In fact, if you select a spot that's got plenty of room for this shrub to spread, it is not likely you'll ever need to prune at all. Single-flowering Japanese kerria grows 4 to 5 feet high and may spread up to 6 feet in width. Grow a solitary plant as an accent or mass several shrubs together for a springtime swath of green and gold.

Oakleaf Hydrangea

P lenty of shade gardening books are devoted solely to those little wildflowers and charming itsy-bitsy plants that will thrive only if your soil is as rich, moist, dark, and crumbly as chocolate cake. A few such plants are included in this book for those lucky souls who are naturally blessed with such soil or who are willing to work hard enough to create it in their shade beds. But for the rest of us, there are bigger, tougher plants like oakleaf hydrangea.

Oakleaf hydrangea is native to many parts of the South, meaning that it grows wild with help from no one. It thrives in woodland soils that are moist or dry. This shade-loving shrub will grow in soil with low pH, high pH, or anything in between. As long as you remember to avoid sites with hot afternoon sun or wet, boggy soil, you're bound to find success with oakleaf hydrangea.

This shrub is as pretty as it is tough. Oakleaf hydrangea earned its name by virtue of its very large leaves with a lobed shape that resemble—you guessed it—oak leaves. The large leaves give oakleaf hydrangea a coarse-textured appearance, making it useful for growing behind more delicate plants. The contrast between fine-texture foliage and this hydrangea's large leaves is quite attractive.

In autumn, oakleaf hydrangea's foliage changes from green to head-turning shades of scarlet, deep red, and purple. But then—sigh—the leaves do fall off, leaving bare sticks all winter long. If this bothers you, plant oakleaf hydrangea where there's a solid year-round background behind it, such as a wall, fence, or evergreen plant. Don't rely on this shrub to add privacy or screen something from view because it won't do either when bare during the winter months.

But the best is yet to come: Spring brings a dramatic show of blossoms, making the winter wait worthwhile. After new leaves appear, oakleaf hydrangea sports creamy panicles of multiple blossoms resembling over-sized vanilla ice cream cones. The light-colored blooms brighten shady beds. The flowers are long-lived, and they have the added feature of turning pink in summer as they fade and dry on the stems. Don't cut spent

---

Hydrangea quercifolia

GETTING ACQUAINTED

Deciduous shrub (bare in winter)

6 to 10 feet high by 3 to 8 feet wide

Large plumes of creamy flowers open in spring, then turn pinkish in summer, and tan in autumn; big leaves turn red and purple in autumn.

Moderate to rapid growth rate

Native

Partial shade; avoid hot afternoon sun

Any soil that's not wet

Good choice for natural areas, edges of woodlands, wildflower gardens, slopes, beside fences or walls, near evergreen plants; looks great beside stonework

Pairs well in fertile, dry soil with eastern hemlock, bluestar, star magnolia, Japanese kerria, redbud, daffodil, periwinkle, Pinxterbloom azalea, dead nettle, beautyberry, Lenten rose, Spanish bluebell, and mondo grass; in moist soil with trillium, rhododendron, bluebells, celandine poppy, Solomon's seal, astilbe, foamflower, windflower, bleeding heart, melampodium, red buckeye, yellow archangel, hosta, and ferns.

Zones 5–9

Oakleaf hydrangea's habit of forming large clumps combined with its informal, irregular shape make it a good choice for planting in large masses beneath trees for a natural look.

OAKLEAF HYDRANGEA'S ENEMIES

Even a plant as easy to grow as this one can fail to thrive if its adversaries gain the upper hand. Keep foes in check for carefree, long-lived, beautiful plants.

ENEMY NUMBER 1: SUN

If leaves wilt regularly or develop a crispy, burned look, then your oakleaf hydrangeas are getting too much sun. Afternoon sun is particularly damaging to oakleaf hydrangeas in those parts of the South where summer blazes and winter is mild.

Solution: Dig up your oakleaf hydrangeas and replant in a shadier location. If you've recently planted them in a spots that's too sunny, it is okay to dig the plants up again regardless of the season, but water regularly to help overcome the trauma of hot-weather transplanting. If shrubs are well established but their shade coverage has been reduced, water as needed to get them through the summer, but wait until plants have shed their leaves in fall to move them.

ENEMY NUMBER 2: MALES OF OUR SPECIES

To make a blatantly sexist observation, men are generally the ones who get pruner-happy and start cutting everything in sight. Oakleaf hydrangeas don't need to be pruned—ever. They're supposed to be freeform, irregularly shaped plants with mounding foliage. And they're supposed to get big, so start them where they've got plenty of room to grow. Chopping off these shrubs at one level or cutting them back in an attempt to form balls or cubes will reduce flowering in addition to ruining the shape of the plant.

Solution: Advice in print equals wisdom, so show the clipper-happy guy at your house this book. While he's looking at it, get all the electric clipping devices out of the garage and give them away. Hand pruners don't make that cool whirring noise so they're less fun to use, which gives your oakleaf hydrangeas a fighting chance.

Okay, there is one exception to the no-pruning rule, but guys, don't think you're off the over-cutting hook. If oakleaf hydrangeas are growing in such dense shade that they've become all leg and no leaf as they lengthen in an attempt to reach some sunlight, it is okay to cut the woody stalks back somewhat. However, it is only worth doing if you also move the plants to a better location. Once they're transplanted, no more pruning.

A

B

C

D

E

F

SHRUBS: SHOWY

G

H

blooms unless you want to dry them for use in arrangements. Otherwise, leave them on plants to enjoy the change of colors from cream to pink to light tan. Collecting a few flowers won't affect the following year's blooming, but don't cut many and don't prune these plants.

Young plants are likely to require supplemental watering during the first growing season, but as long as oakleaf hydrangeas are protected from hours of hot sun, you won't have to do anything to them once roots become established. Older plants are quite drought tolerant. A really bad summer of high temperatures and no rain can leave this shrub looking sad, but expect a comeback when rains return. A little merciful watering helps, too.

(A) Long bundles of beady green buds open to form elegant cones of white flowers in summer.
(B) The blossoms of oakleaf hydrangea are long lasting and turn pink by summer's end.
(C) In autumn, the pink hues fade to tan.
(D) The foliage of oakleaf hydrangea takes center stage in autumn, when leaves turn shades of red, purple, and burgundy.
(E) To speed the growth of oakleaf hydrangeas in poor soils, add compost or leaf humus to holes before planting.
(F) Snowflake® is a selection bred for its ruffled double blossoms. This named variety is lovely, but plant it within reach of a hose, as it isn't quite as drought tolerant as the parent species. This cultivar is not to be confused with 'Snow Queen', which has single blossoms.
(G) Oakleaf hydrangea makes a lovely warm-season backdrop to garden rooms.
(H) The aptly named oakleaf hydrangea grows large leaves in varying lobed shapes. Foliage drops in winter, revealing bare trunks. Some homeowners find the naked stems objectionable, while others enjoy the peeling bark.

Rhododendron periclymenoides

Also sold as Pinxter flower,
Rhododendron nudiflorum

GETTING ACQUAINTED

Deciduous shrub (bare in winter)

4 to 6 feet high by 3 to 4 feet wide

Delicate clusters of dainty flowers open in
spring in shades of pink and white

Moderate rate of growth

Native

Partial shade

Moist, well-drained soil; will adapt to dry, rocky
soil; not for alkaline or wet soil

Good choice for natural areas, stream banks,
woodlands, and the fronts of shady beds;
grow in masses or as singular accent plants;
adds interest to groundcover beds.

Pairs well with hosta, holly fern, Japanese
painted fern, trillium, windflower, Lenten
rose, Solomon's seal, Virginia sweetspire,
smilax, yellow archangel, bluestar, bluebells,
fothergilla, foamflower, star magnolia, and
hydrangeas; grow in front of eastern hemlock, pieris, camellia, or rhododendron

Zones 4–9

The luscious pink, honeysuckle-like blossoms
of Pinxterbloom azaleas attract butterflies and
hummingbirds.

Pinxterbloom Azalea

After standing bare and forgotten all winter, the Pinxterbloom azalea becomes quite glamorous in mid to late spring. That's when blossoms open in fluffy clusters at the ends of slender gray branches. Flower petals curl back ever so slightly, showing off long, lashlike filaments that give blooms a decidedly coy appearance. Still-colorful spent flowers often dangle before dropping, adding to the plant's dainty look.

Pinxterbloom flowers are usually pink, although blossom hues range among plants from pale blush and nearly white to cotton candy and rich rose. The tubular blossoms often take on a two-toned look as the deeper color of the tube is highlighted by the pastel shades of the open flower. Unlike most of the azaleas you'll find for sale, the Pinxterbloom is deciduous, loosing all of its leaves each autumn. It also blooms later than many azaleas. In the South, leaves may appear on Pinxterblooms just before flowers do or they may emerge at about the same time. The bright green new leaves show off the rosy blossoms even more. Flowers are fragrant and attract hummingbirds as well as several species of butterflies.

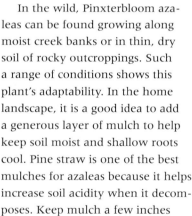

In the wild, Pinxterbloom azaleas can be found growing along moist creek banks or in thin, dry soil of rocky outcroppings. Such a range of conditions shows this plant's adaptability. In the home landscape, it is a good idea to add a generous layer of mulch to help keep soil moist and shallow roots cool. Pine straw is one of the best mulches for azaleas because it helps increase soil acidity when it decomposes. Keep mulch a few inches away from the trunks of azaleas. Water young plants lightly on a regular basis to keep roots evenly moist. Avoid binge watering, which can allow water to collect in the holes around roots, drowning them. Older plants adapt to less water, especially when mulched well and protected from western sun. In naturally moist conditions, Pinxterbloom azaleas send up shoots from the roots to form colonies of plants. This habit is called "suck-

A

ering" by those who don't want it to occur, and "naturalizing" by those who find it desirable, so take your pick.

The best place to add Pinxterbloom azalea to your landscape is an area that receives dappled sun most of the day. A location that's shaded by high tree canopies, such as tall pines, is ideal. Pinxterbloom azaleas need shade to keep them from scorching in hot summer sun, but a good dose of sunlight is necessary for flowering. If your garden doesn't have filtered shade that lets limited sunlight through, choose a spot that receives sun in the morning but is shaded in the afternoon. Pinxterblooms grown in dense shade will not flower well and will eventually lean toward sunlight.

Pinxterblooms grow tall, so don't try to prune them into compact little shrubs. The natural form of the plant is graceful, open, and airy. If you want, you can remove the lower branches of your Pinxterbloom azalea to shape it like a little tree. The goal is to expose the trunks a little, so don't go crazy with the clippers. Once you've got pruners in hand, the urge to go ahead and trim the plant's canopy is a powerful one, but fight it you must. If you give in, you'll end up without any flowers on your Pinxterbloom the following spring. Shaping it like a lollipop will also ruin the plant's delicate form.

B

(A) In shady spots, Pinxterbloom azalea underplanted with variegated hosta makes an eye-catching combination that's hard to beat.
(B) Despite its delicate blossoms, this shrub is quite cold tolerant. Pinxterbloom azaleas lose their leaves in winter, unlike the evergreen Southern Indica.

PROPER PLANTING OF AZALEAS

Like other azaleas, Pinxterbloom demands good drainage to thrive. It is critical to avoid planting these shrubs too deeply—excess soil around the stems can cause crown rot. And shallow feeder roots, characteristic of all azaleas, need to grow near the soil's surface, not buried down deep. The secret of success is to use a technique known as "planting high" when planting any kind of azalea. First, dig the planting hole twice as wide as the nursery container. Next, form a firm little mound in the bottom of the planting hole. Position the new plant minus its pot on the mound within the hole so that the top of the rootball is about 1 inch higher than the undisturbed soil of the surrounding bed. (If it sits too low, remove the plant and increase the mound.) Use a trowel to gently loosen some of the roots that remain visibly wound tightly in the pot's shape. Backfill around the rootball using a mixture of one part soil removed from the hole and one part organic matter. Keep the rootball in its slightly protruding position. Mulch a wide circle that covers the rootball but doesn't touch the shrub's trunks. Planting high may seem odd the first time you do it, but this trick will ensure that your new azalea doesn't settle too deeply in its planting hole.

EVERGREEN AZALEAS

Though Pinxterblooms are bare in winter, there are plenty of non-native azaleas that offer year-round greenery and a wide range of blossom colors. Buy them in bloom to get the color you like. If you can kick-start your self control, limit your purchases to a single color (many azalea flower hues clash with one another). Consider the color of your home when making your selection, especially if your new azaleas will grow beside it. Some of the strongest blossom hues are only suitable for planting close to neutral or dark-colored houses. Red brick is particularly hard to complement with any azalea color except white. Consider the eventual size of different choices, too, so your azaleas won't block your windows.

EVERGREEN AZALEA	EVENTUAL SIZE	BLOOM TIME
'Gumpo' (Satsuki)	1 to 2 feet high and wide	summer
Encore® series	3 to 5 feet high and wide	spring and summer/fall
Glen Dale hybrids	3 to 5 feet high and wide	spring (cold tolerant)
Kurume series	3 to 5 feet high and wide	spring
Southern Indica	6 to 10 feet high and wide	spring

The best time to prune evergreen azaleas is when they're in full bloom. You don't have to worry about cutting off next year's flower buds. You're also less likely to go overboard and cut too much. Remove leggy branches by reaching inside the plant with hand pruners to trim long, brown stems. If cuts are hidden by flowers and foliage, you've done it correctly. Enjoy the long-lasting cut stems of azalea flowers indoors in a vase of water.

Pinxterbloom azaleas thrive in the high shade of mature trees. But it is important to avoid planting azaleas of any kind within the shade of maples. The shallow roots of these trees extend as wide as their canopies do. In a competition for water, maple roots will win and azaleas will loose. Dogwoods are also shallow-rooted, making them a poor close companion for azaleas, too.

Virginia Sweetspire

Wet soil is off-limits for so many plants, you may wonder if you've got to abandon damp areas of your landscape to whatever weeds happen to appear. But fear not, Virginia sweetspire is here. This plucky shrub thrives in moisture. Plant it in low spots that puddle regularly after a rain shower or a sprinkler system has run. You can also grow Virginia sweetspire along creek banks, beside ponds and swales, and in bogs, moist beds, and woodlands. Boasting late spring to early summer flowers and autumn color, this plant is an attractive problem-solver.

But don't turn the page if the soil in your garden is average to dry. Though it is likely to grow more slowly—and less likely to spread from a single plant into a small colony of shrubs—the ever-adaptable Virginia sweetspire can grow in dry soil, too. Regular watering will help get young plants off to a good start, but established plants are surprisingly drought tolerant.

Virginia sweetspire's creamy flowers arrive in late spring to early summer after plants have fully leafed out. Most shrubs that produce long spikes of flowers hold them erect, like candles, but sweetspire blossoms add an interesting twist as they turn in different directions, like so many big, fuzzy, white caterpillars. 'Henry's Garnet' is a named selection of Virginia sweetspire featuring blooms that often reach 6 inches in length. If you can find it, buy it. Plants simply tagged as Virginia sweetspire (instead of 'Henry's Garnet') grow pretty flowers, too, but blossoms are likely to be closer to 4 inches in length. All sweetspire flowers are pleasantly fragrant.

Henry's Garnet sweetspire grows wider than it does tall. It matures at about 4 to 5 feet high and 6 feet wide, whereas other selections of Virginia sweetspire may as tall as 8 to 10 feet with a spread of 5 to 6 feet. Because of its denser, broader form, Henry's Garnet sweetspire is particularly well suited for setting groups of plants together in a mass or informal hedge.

GETTING ACQUAINTED

Deciduous shrub (bare in winter)

3 to 4 feet high by 6 to 8 feet wide

Long white flowers cover shrubs in summer; leaves turn purplish red in autumn

Rapid rate of growth (moderate in dry soils)

Insect and disease resistant

Native

Partial shade to all-day sun

Moist to wet soil is preferable, but will also grow in dry soil

Good choice for damp areas, fronts of shady beds, informal hedges, natural areas, woodland gardens, slopes, creek banks, and pond sides; pretty beside patios

Pairs well in wet soil with bluestar, smilax, and cardinal flower; in moist soil with foamflower, bleeding heart, melampodium, Solomon's seal, Pinxterbloom azalea, hosta, hydrangeas, pieris, red buckeye, yellow archangel, and astilbe; and in dry soil with fothergilla, liriope, aucuba, mondo grass, camellia, Lenten rose, beautyberry, leatherleaf mahonia, star magnolia, and in front of eastern hemlock

Zones 5–9

Native throughout much of the Southeastern United States, *Itea virginica* flowers in late spring to early summer. If leaves of plants grown in soils with high pH turn yellow, provide a dose of magnesium sulfate or elemental sulfur.

A

B

All Virginia sweetspires are bare in winter, so don't plant them where you need to block views year-round. Before the foliage drops, the leaves turn a pretty purplish red to ruby red, with Henry's Garnet sweetspire providing the most reliable color.

Virginia sweetspire can thrive in full sun when it is grown in damp spots or cooler regions of the South. But dry soil and long, hot summers make partially shaded locations better choices for growing these shrubs for many homeowners. Avoid all-day shade—sweetspires may grow there, but flowering will be reduced and autumn color tends to be disappointing in deeply shaded locations. Beds that receive a half-day's sun or all-day dappled sun are fine. Because it isn't necessary to shield Virginia sweetspires from afternoon sun, you can plant them where sunrays reach the plants in either morning or afternoon. In fact, a dose of direct afternoon sunlight may produce the best autumn color in shrubs grown in partial shade.

A SMALLER SWEETSPIRE

Little Henry® is a compact version of Henry's Garnet sweetspire. This junior selection grows just 2.0 to 2.5 feet high and 3 feet wide, making a dense, spreading shrub. Grows in partial shade or full sun. The foliage of Little Henry® turns bright red in autumn. Spring flowers are sweetly scented.

(A) Virginia sweetspire thrives in soil that's too wet for many plants. This shrub may sucker in damp soil, spreading to form colonies of plants
(B) 'Henry's Garnet' is a named selection of Virginia sweetspire with a solid reputation for purplish red to ruby foliage in autumn.

SHRUBS: SHOWY

Evergreen Shrubs

Aucuba

Aucuba japonica

Also sold as Japanese aucuba, Japanese laurel

GETTING ACQUAINTED

Evergreen shrub

4 to 12 feet high by 3 to 8 feet wide

Glossy foliage is available in a range of colors, from solid deep green to golden speckles to yellow blotches

Moderate rate of growth

All-day shade to partial shade

Any soil except wet

Tolerates pollution and dry soil

Good choice for shady beds, foundation plantings, large courtyards, patios, low decks, formal gardens, informal landscapes, background plantings, or use as an accent in a groundcover bed

Pairs well with fothergilla, bluestar, smilax, windflower, periwinkle, Virginia sweetspire, hosta, daffodil, mondo grass, liriope, dead nettle, holly fern, leatherleaf mahonia, Japanese kerria, caladium, mahonia, periwinkle, and melampodium

Zones 7–10

The thick-leaved aucuba will grow in the sunshine in cooler regions, but it must be protected from the hot sun of the South. Sun damage causes leaves to blacken.

With so many shrubs for sale that prefer partial shade, it can be challenging to find something that thrives in dense, all-day shade. Fortunately, aucuba grows as well in full shade as it does in partial shade. This glossy-leaved shrub has two main requirements, and shade is at the top of the list. The other necessity is well-drained soil. Such a combination of desires makes aucuba a good choice for growing in the shadows cast by large shade trees, where tree roots provide stiff competition for soil moisture. Many plants can't grow in such conditions, but aucuba can.

Because aucuba is never without leaves, it helps keep your landscape from appearing empty when other plants are bare in winter or simply past their peak. Aucuba comes in a variety of leaf patterns. 'Gold Dust', sometimes sold as 'Variegata', is one of the most common selections and features golden speckles on green leaves. It is a nice contrast to the plain greens of many in other shade lovers, such as English ivy, mondo grass, ferns, and liriope. Pepper Pot® aucuba leaves are gently splattered with even tinier gold dots than those of 'Gold Dust'. The subtle pattern of Pepper Pot® adds interest without distraction.

Other variegated aucuba leaves may prove to be too strong for most compositions. I particularly dislike the screaming yellow blotches of a selection named 'Picturata'. It always looks chlorotic to me, like a shrub that's badly in need of fertilizer. My personal prejudice against glaring yellow foliage also prevents me from including 'Sulphur' in landscape designs; I don't find the yellow-edged foliage attractive. 'Goldiana' combines golden freckles with the yellow splotches, whereas 'Goldilocks' and

A

B

C

'Crotonifolia' both feature bright green leaves streaked with yellow—not my taste. While I concede that such varieties have their uses, I believe that one of these strongly colored plants per landscape is usually plenty.

Plain green aucuba, often sold under the cultivar names 'Viridis', 'Macrophylla', 'Longifolia', or 'Serratifolia', is an underused shrub. Though it lacks the pizzazz of the colored-leaf varieties, that's exactly the point. The foliage won't clash with any color scheme, so these selections are

(A) 'Gold Dust' is variegated selection that's commonly for sale. You can clip foliage for an attractive, long-lasting addition to flower arrangements. Stems set in water may produce roots. You can grow these plantlets in your own landscape, or give them away to friends and neighbors to start their own aucubas.

(B) To enjoy shiny red berries, you'll have to be lucky enough to have a female plant with a male aucuba in the vicinity.

(C) Snow isn't as damaging to aucuba as ice is. The best place to include these shrubs is along the southern or western exposures of your property in the shade. Avoiding morning rays helps frozen aucubas thaw slowly, minimizing cold damage.

AVOIDING PROBLEMS

Aucuba grown in the right setting is a lovely and carefree plant. Taking the following precautions can prevent problems that plague some aucubas.

MULCH

Do not pile soil or mulch around trunks. In fact, it is a good idea to keep soil 6 inches away from trunks.

FERTILIZER

Feed shrubs sparingly with an acid fertilizer only when necessary to green up yellowing foliage that is beyond characteristic yellow leaf patterns. (You may never need to feed your aucuba.) Excessive fertilizer is damaging to these shrubs. When you must feed an aucuba, do so in late spring and don't apply fertilizer near the trunks.

SOIL PROBLEMS

To avoid trouble with nematodes or wet soil, don't plant aucubas where rhododendrons, azaleas, or other aucubas have failed earlier. Water young plants when newly planted and during hot droughts, but don't water established aucubas unless they wilt. Dry soil is better than too-wet soil.

COLD

In regions with harsh winters, plant aucuba where it is protected from blasts of extremely cold air. Plants grown beside paving or walls are often warmer than those grown in exposed areas. To help aucuba bounce back from a severe freeze, plant it where eastern morning rays can't strike still-frozen plants. Sun on frozen aucubas can cause branch tips and leaves to blacken. Frozen aucubas that thaw slowly rarely suffer cold damage.

Frozen aucuba leaves appear wilted. Plants recover well if they thaw slowly.

PRUNING

Trimming to control the size of plants should be done in mid-spring, after the last freeze. That's the best time to cut away branches blackened by cold, too. Don't prune aucuba in late summer or autumn, as doing so will encourage new growth that's susceptible to cold damage in winter.

Prune to control size as needed by reaching into plants to make cuts. You may notice that tips of all branches are green, an identifying characteristic of aucuba.

great for planting in shady spots beside your house. Green aucubas also showcase brightly colored plants without competing with them for attention. Green aucuba leaves are dark and glossy, attractive in their own right.

Though aucuba prefers slightly acidic soil, it will adapt to alkaline soil when grown in enough shade. Wet soil can cause roots to rot. In areas with heavy clay soil, grow aucuba in raised beds, on slopes, or in large containers. Unless your native soil is already sandy, it is a good idea to mix some sand or gypsum into soil at planting to improve drainage. Including large particles of organic matter such as chunky compost or pine bark is prudent, too, as this will enrich the soil in addition to helping drainage. Make sure the top of the new plant's rootball sits level with adjacent undisturbed soil. It you put the plant in the hole and it sits too low, remove the shrub and mound some soil in the bottom of the hole to raise the rootball.

Camellia

Camellia japonica

Also sold as common camellia, Japanese camellia

When a Southerner says, "japonica," that means camellia. Though there are thousands of plants with *japonica* included in their botanical names—indicating a Japanese origin—only *Camellia japonica* has earned such shorthand familiarity among gardeners. This, no doubt, is an indication of how beloved a shrub camellia is in the South.

If you're new to the region or new to gardening, you may not be on such a species-name basis, yourself. But get to know this plant, and you'll find yourself charmed as well. The flowers are incredible. The foliage is deep, forest green. The plants are effortlessly long-lived when grown in the right conditions. Perhaps best of all, the blossoms appear in winter.

In zone 9, coastal areas, and the lower half of zone 8, camellia blossoms in winter are as reliable as mosquitoes in summer. Large, fat buds form on the tips of branches by late summer. They swell throughout autumn and burst into bloom sometime after Christmas, around February to early March in many areas. Each flower sits in a nest of rich, green leaves. Blooms are large, up to 5 inches across in some selections, with an average size of 3 inches in diameter. In zone 7 and the colder parts of zone 8, flowers opened by warm spells during the winter months may be browned by sudden temperature dips. Though it is a shame to lose the blossoms, the plants are not harmed. It is well worth the risk of damaged flowers to grow camellias in these areas, as there will be years when the floral show plays uninterrupted. Besides, you can always pick plenty of camellia blooms to enjoy indoors when a threatening cold snap looms. For the plants themselves to suffer serious cold damage, tem-

GETTING ACQUAINTED

Evergreen shrub

6 to 8 feet high and wide; may reach 12 feet with age

Large flowers with waxy petals open in winter; dark green leaves are attractive year-round

Slow rate of growth

Partial shade

Well-drained, acidic soil

Good choice for courtyards, entry areas, foundation plantings, backgrounds of seasonal flower beds, shady beds, and spots where you can see them from inside your home; thrives in coastal gardens

Pairs well with pieris, rhododendron, Pinxterbloom azalea, hydrangeas, Virginia sweetspire, fothergilla, daffodil, Spanish bluebell, smilax, bluestar, Japanese kerria, climbing hydrangea, and caladium

Zones 7–9

Camellias have glossy green leaves year-round, they bloom in late winter, and they're long-lived. Perhaps the only reason camellias aren't found in every Southern landscape is the fact that these shrubs grow slowly.

SHRUBS: EVERGREEN

perature drops must be sustained below 0°F for a good six hours or so. Fortunately, such tacky weather is rare in most of the South.

Camellia flowers are available in different forms. There are single flowers that have open ruffled petals and noticeable yellow stamens. There are semi-double flowers that have more petals but are still open enough to show the stamens. Then there's the formal double, a perfect arrangement of tightly nested petals. This includes my favorite camellia, a shell-pink formal double called 'Pink Perfection'. Other camellia bloom types are named after flowers they resemble: the rose form, peony form, and anemone form. There are many dozens of named selections in a wide range of solid and mixed colors, so you're bound to find something you like. The luscious blossoms of camellias are a little illusory—I've heard people exclaim over their fragrance even though most camellias bear no scent at all. The mistake is understandable. Camellia flowers certainly look as though they would smell wonderful. And other sweetly scented bloomers, such as paperwhite narcissus and osmanthus, flower at the same time as camellias do, releasing a deceptive fragrance. (A selection known as 'Fragrant Pink' is one of the few sweet-smelling camellias.)

Camellias need acidic soil that drains well. Don't even attempt to grow this shrub in highly alkaline soil. The sandy soils of Florida, southern Georgia, and the coastal South are ideally suited for camellias—but don't plant them at the beach, as camellias are not salt tolerant. You can grow camellias successfully in clay if the soil is naturally acidic and you take care to improve drainage by preparing a raised bed and adding plenty of sand or gypsum and large-particle organic matter to the soil mix.

A shady spot is the best site to add camellias to your landscape. Like azaleas, camellias thrive in the high shade of tall pines. All-day dappled shade or areas that are shaded in the afternoon are good locations for camellias. Morning sun is agreeable. Aged camellias can be found thriving in the full brunt of hot sun, but such plants have well established root systems and thick canopies that help shade the roots. When starting young camellias, partial shade is your best bet. Mix rich organic matter such as compost with soil at planting. It is wise to invest in a large camellia, as this shrub grows slowly.

Happy camellias flourish with natural rainfall only, but it is a good idea to water plants that are less than three years old on a somewhat regular basis. Feed after flowering with an acid fertilizer that lists azaleas and camellias on the label, especially if foliage yellows. If leaves remain a healthy deep green and your plant is thriving, you can skip fertilizing.

(A) Flowering can be incredibly dense on older camellia shrubs.

(B) Camellia blossoms are available in hundreds of color combinations and petal arrangements. Peony forms such as this one are packed with petals.

(c) For a simply elegant centerpiece in a hurry, pick a single camellia flower and float it in a crystal bowl half-filled with water.

(D) The cultivar 'Mathotiana' is one of many camellias that thrives in hot, shady environments. *Photo courtesy of Magnolia Gardens Nursery*

(E) Formal double camellia flowers feature nested petals that open from the outside of the blossom first.

(F) When you must prune a camellia, do so immediately after flowering finishes to avoid cutting off buds of next year's blossoms. You can train camellias into tree forms by removing a small number of lower branches to expose the trunks.

(G) There's no need to ever chop trunks or savagely cut camellia canopies. Trim branches only on occasion as needed to control size, remove dead wood, or eliminate stray shoots. Always reach into the plant to make hidden cuts.

Mahonia bealei

Not to be confused with Oregon grape holly, *Mahonia aquifolium*

GETTING ACQUAINTED

Evergreen shrub

4 to 6 high by 3 to 4 wide

Yellow winter flowers are followed by grapelike clusters of bluish black berries

Slow rate of growth

Resistant to insects and disease

Drought tolerant

All-day or half-day's shade

Any soil that's not wet

Prune stalks by thirds every few years to keep plants bushy

Good choice for narrow spaces, foundations, courtyards, niches in architecture, tucking beside walls or paving, and growing in the background of shady beds

Don't plant in woodlands, where this shrub may become invasive

Pairs well with aucuba, mondo grass, liriope, periwinkle, yellow archangel, dead nettle, bluestar, Virginia sweetspire, fothergilla, daffodil, holly fern, gooseneck loosestrife, and windflower

Zones 5–8

Yellow winter flowers of leatherleaf mahonia are undeterred by freezing temperatures. Blooms open from the bottom of stiff tassels first.

Leatherleaf Mahonia

Leatherleaf mahonia is one of those plants you probably think you hate. That's because when left unpruned, this shrub gets gawky, stalky, and ugly. But hey, you wouldn't look so great if you never cut your hair, so give this plant a chance. A little grooming is all leatherleaf mahonia needs to become a valued member of your landscape.

Pruning this woody shrub isn't hard to do. About every third year or so, cut one-third of the stalks to reduce them by one-third of their height. Cut another third of the canes to make them two-thirds shorter than they were growing. And leave the other third of the stalks untouched. The main trick to pruning leatherleaf mahonia is to randomly select the stalks for cutting. You don't want to chop off all the canes on one side of the plant and leave a bunch of tall ones in the middle. Instead, pick stalks throughout the plant to prune. The idea is to stair-step the cuts throughout the cluster of stems so you end up with a nice, bushy plant instead of a collection of woody stems with a few leaves at the top. With proper pruning, leatherleaf mahonia can be kept anywhere from 4 to 6 feet high and about 3 to 4 feet wide.

Here's why the pruning lesson is worth your while. Leatherleaf mahonia doesn't just tolerate shade, it actually loves it. That's a big plus. Another selling point—leatherleaf mahonia is tough. It isn't picky about soil, it tolerates drought, and it is hard to kill. You won't want to plant this shrub in standing water or full sun, but that's not a very long list of restrictions.

Leatherleaf mahonia is an excellent choice for narrow areas. Remember, pruning is necessary to encourage this plant to grow a bushy shape; its natural habit is an upright cluster of stems. Like nandina (*Nandina domestica*), leatherleaf mahonia doesn't produce any horizontal

(A) Flowers give way to large, blue-green berries that ripen to blue-black fruits.
(B) Clusters of leatherleaf mahonia's mature berries attract birds.

branches. You can plant leatherleaf mahonia in restricted space between the driveway and the house and you won't have to worry that it is going to get so broad that it will crowd the driveway. The roots won't harm the paving or foundation, either.

As if these aren't enough reasons to make you feel more kindly toward this misunderstood plant, consider this: Leatherleaf mahonia blooms in winter. When you're sick of gray days and true spring is still months away, this shrub comes to the rescue. Its blossoms aren't knock-you-dead, glorious-flower-show types, but they are flowers nonetheless and they do brighten the winter landscape. Mops of long-lived flowers resembling yellow tassels decorate mahonia from January through February. These cheerful splashes of color contrast nicely with the shrub's broad, blue-green foliage. Snow and ice don't deter flowering or damage blossoms.

By the time high spring rolls around and more dramatic flowers are in their glory, leatherleaf mahonia's yellow blooms will have faded from memory. But next thing you know, they've been replaced with attractive clusters of blue-green berries. The fruits ripen to blue-black and resemble large, waxy grapes. Friends will start asking just what are those interesting plants in your garden. Wild birds will enjoy the bounty, too.

As with many shade plants, texture is an important characteristic of this shrub. Aptly named, leatherleaf mahonia produces big, leathery leaflets that resemble holly leaves. The foliage is considered coarse-textured in appearance because the leaves are large. And because coarse-textured foliage is attractive when contrasted against fine-textured foliage, you can look like you really know what you're doing when you pair leatherleaf mahonia with smaller-leaved plants such as ferns or mondo grass. Mahonia never goes bare, so it offers a year-round presence in the landscape.

MAHONIA CARE

PLANTING

Leatherleaf mahonia thrives in all-day shade or half-day's shade. In hotter climates (zone 8 and coastal regions), you'll want to protect this plant from afternoon sun. Hot, western rays in these areas can cause the edges of the leaves to turn crispy and brown.

PRUNING

Reach into plants to remove selected stalks at different heights with hand pruners or loppers. Don't try to prune leatherleaf mahonia into any kind of geometrical shape, and don't flattop the plant by cutting all the stalks off at the same level (see page 90).

Pruning encourages leaf growth in leatherleaf mahonias. The plant on the left needs to be cut by thirds to make it bushy, like the mahonia on the right. Fortunately, pruning mahonia is easy to do.

REHABILITATING

Don't dig up and discard established but leggy leatherleaf mahonias just because they've been neglected. Give them a proper pruning and wait a season before passing judgment on this useful shade-loving shrub. Plants look a lot better when woody stalks are replaced with foliage after pruning.

Pieris japonica

Also sold as Japanese pieris, andromeda, lily-of-the-valley shrub

GETTING ACQUAINTED

Evergreen shrub

8 to 10 feet high and wide

Attractive in all seasons; showy spring flowers drape over plants; new foliage is reddish and attractive; autumn fruit persists through winter

Slow rate of growth

Partial shade to all-day shade; protect from hot afternoon sun

Moist, fertile soil that's well drained; acidic soil is best

Good choice for woodlands, natural areas, Japanese gardens, and background plantings; use to screen views and divide space into outdoor rooms; include in foundation plantings only near tall, blank walls to avoid blocking windows

Pairs well with rhododendron, Pinxterbloom azalea, Japanese kerria, Virginia sweetspire, fothergilla, daffodil, camellia, foamflower, astilbe, bleeding heart, Solomon's seal, red buckeye, yellow archangel, liriope, mondo grass, periwinkle, and tall pines

Zones 5–8

Though it grows slowly, pieris becomes a large shrub that's useful for defining spaces within the landscape.

Pieris

Most homeowners have plenty of openings for a shrub that stays green all year and grows in the shade. Pieris is a strong candidate if you've got average to fertile garden soil in a spot that's not too difficult to keep reasonably moist. Pieris thrives in shadowy spots, where soil may not be heated by sun to become bone dry. Young plants need regular water to thrive, but older plants adapt to drier conditions. A generous layer of mulch also helps keep these pretty plants happy.

Pieris is a dense shrub with large leaves that grow in attractive tiers. Its large size and evergreen foliage make pieris perfect for blocking views, adding privacy, and defining outdoor rooms within your landscape. This shrub grows slowly, however, so don't expect a quick screen. The upside of slow growth is that pruning is not usually necessary. Grow pieris in all-day shade or in locations where it is protected from hot afternoon sun that slants from the west. In areas with harsh seasonal winds, plant pieris in protected locations where it won't become dried out by blustery weather.

Long tassels of creamy flowers cover pieris in spring. The blooms are strung together like tiny Chinese paper lanterns, and they last for weeks. The shape of the flowers reminds some of lily-of-the-valley blossoms, giving pieris the nickname lily-of-the-valley shrub, though the blooms of this large bush lack the famous sweet scent of the little groundcover's flowers. You can enjoy pieris flowers without any effort, or you can take the time to remove spent blossoms to increase and prolong flowering. Buds for next spring's show form by midsummer. If you must trim pieris, do so immediately after flowering ceases or you'll cut off next year's blossoms. It is better to plant this shrub where it has plenty of room and skip pruning altogether. Or, choose a named cultivar that stays small. Flowers yield reddish brown capsules borne on chains in autumn that persist through winter.

A

B

Newly emerging leaves are another attractive feature of pieris. Fresh growth shows up coppery red to bronze and is quite noticeable against older, greener leaves. Foliage is thick and shiny and grows in a whorled arrangement around stems.

Pieris prefers acidic soil but tolerates alkalinity better than previously believed. However, it is a good idea to be diligent about fertilizing pieris grown in high pH soil to improve acidity. In areas with extremely alkaline soil, mountain pieris (*Pieris floribunda*) is a better choice. Though it is not quite as showy as its Japanese cousin, due to smaller flowers that don't drape as gracefully, mountain pieris is tougher. Lacebugs and limestone soils are not problematic for *Pieris floribunda*. This species will eventually grow about 6 feet tall.

(A) The resulting red-brown fruit is a subtle attraction in autumn.
(B) Pieris plants are covered with unusual chains of blossoms in spring.

LACEBUG CONTROL

When this shade-lover receives too much hot sun, it struggles to grow. Such stress makes pieris more susceptible to lacebugs, a pest that damages and discolors the foliage. Severe infestations may require several doses of chemical spray labeled for use against these pests. For organic control, spray plants with insecticidal soap, taking care to soak the undersides of leaves as well as the tops.

You can prevent most lacebug attacks by providing pieris with good growing conditions. Choose shady locations away from afternoon summer sun. Amend soil during planting with plenty of large-particle organic matter to add nutrients and improve drainage. Reapply mulch before hot weather arrives to keeps roots cool and moist (but don't pile mulch around trunks). Feed your pieris each spring immediately after blooming ceases with a high-acid fertilizer, such as azalea/camellia food. Water the plants during droughts. All of these simple tasks help keep pieris shrubs robust, reducing their susceptibility to lacebugs.

NAMED SELECTIONS

'PURITY': very long white flowers; grows about 4 feet high
'MOUNTAIN FIRE': new growth is an exceptionally vivid orange-red
'DOROTHY WYCOFF': buds are red; flowers are light pink
'VALLEY VALENTINE': red buds open to deep pink blossoms

Rhododendron catawbiense
and hybrids

Also sold as Catawba hybrid
rhododendron

Rhododendron

GETTING ACQUAINTED

Evergreen shrub

10 to 12 feet high and wide

Thick leathery green leaves give plants a layered look; large clusters of flowers open in
late spring to early summer; available in a
range of blossom colors

Slow rate of growth (grows moderately faster
in ideal soil)

Partial shade to all-day shade

Moist, well-drained soil with high organic content; soil must be acidic, not for alkaline soil

Good choice for screening views, adding privacy, and for providing a background for
deciduous shrubs and perennials; plant in
shady beds, along edges of woodlands, in
natural areas, and to hide high foundations

Pairs well with bleeding heart, bluestar,
Solomon's seal, trillium, melampodium,
smilax, Japanese maple, periwinkle,
camellia, pieris, star magnolia, redbud,
holly fern, hosta, liriope, mondo grass,
yellow archangel, and fothergilla; provides
a nice background for beautyberry, hydrangeas, foamflower, Lenten rose, Japanese
painted fern, Pinxterbloom azalea, and
Japanese kerria; good in front of eastern
hemlock

Zones 4–8 (excluding warmest parts of zone 8)

The rhododendron draws a clear, neat line in the landscape between the bold and the gaudy. Bold is big but tasteful, occasionally showy but always durable. Gaudy is bright, fleeting, and fancy. I admit to seasonal seduction by quite a few gaudy plants—creeping phlox heads the list—but my respect for big, bold rhododendrons continues to grow, as do the rhodies growing outside my study window.

The plain green leaves of the rhododendron are reliable all year, never disappearing, always cloaking the plant's bony brown branches. It is the boldness, not the color, of rhododendron foliage that is valuable. The leaves' large size, leathery thickness, and interesting arrangement in flat, circular layers—like the giant green petals of some strange flower—give the rhododendron year-round beauty. Shrubs that go bare in winter and perennials that disappear completely until the warm months are not missed as badly when rhododendrons are nearby to provide an evergreen framework. It is also important to note that the seasonally ornamental features of other plants—flowers, colorful leaves, or fine textures—seem even prettier when showcased against a backdrop of rich, green rhododendrons.

Late spring to early summer is the rhododendron's time to take the stage. Fat buds, perching in the centers of radiating leaves, open to become big bunches of flowers known as trusses. Each truss is an oversized corsage, a globe of petals pinned to a nest of greenery. True *Rhododendron catawbiense* blossoms are lavender or pinkish purple, whereas hybrids flower in a range of whites, pinks, lavenders, purples, reds, and even yellow, making it easy to find a rhododendron that complements the color of your home. Shopping for these

Rhododendron planted in front of eastern hemlock
is a classic combination for areas of the South that
see cold winters regularly.

A

B

C

D

E

F

(A) Native Catawba rhododendrons are covered with pinkish purple globes of flowers in spring. Blossom time depends upon temperature, and rhodies in the mountains bloom later than those at lower elevations.

(B) Plants with this flower color may be sold as 'Roseum Elegans' or simply as *Rhododendron catawbiense*.

(C) Bright petals emerge from fat buds.

(D) Hybrid selections expand the color palette to include bright pink.

(E) Soft white blooms blushed with pink show up well in the shade.

(F) Though rhododendrons are prized for their flowers, the evergreen foliage alone would make them worth planting. Here, they're well placed at the foot of a high porch. The presence of these large green shrubs is particularly valuable in winter, when other plants are bare.

PRUNING RHODODENDRONS

Have rubbing alcohol handy when pruning rhododendrons. Sterilizing blades between cuts will prevent the spread of disease. This is particularly important when removing dead or dieing branches. Always cut at least an inch below unhealthy wood so you're cutting into green, undamaged wood. This helps keep pruning tools clean. Dispose of cuttings off-site; never compost rhododendron debris.

Severely withered branches and dead foliage hanging on stems often indicates a fungal problem common to rhododendrons.

When you see branches like this one, it's time to act. Remove damaged portions of the plant. Spray affected rhododendrons in spring with fungicide containing basic copper sulfate, repeating the application two more times, two weeks apart.

Make cuts by reaching into plants and slicing through the wood with a single, angled cut made by a sharp blade and adequate force. (You may have to use long-handled loppers for good leverage.) Never saw along a cut with an undersized pruning tool. The resulting jagged cut is an invitation to pests and disease. You can cut away leggy branches to keep shrubs thick and full and to control the height. Or, let rhododendrons grow naturally to form tall, sculptural specimens that may eventually resemble little trees.

WILTING

When rhododendron leaves droop in summer, plants are hot. Provide moisture but don't drown these shrubs in an attempt to perk up the foliage; it will

This rhododendron isn't thirsty, it's cold. Leaves straighten up when temperatures rise.

take a drop in temperature to do that. Rhododendron leaves also curl and droop in below-freezing weather. Plants are not injured and will assume their regular appearance when the cold snap ends.

MOUNTAIN LAUREL

If you've got the right conditions for growing rhododendron, then you've also got a good setting for the native mountain laurel, *Kalmia latifolia*. Soil, moisture, and shade requirements are very similar for these two flowering evergreen shrubs. Mountain laurels even bloom in late spring to early summer, around the same time rhododendrons do. But mountain laurel flowers have their own look: white cups neatly embroidered with dark pink. Cups are borne in clusters on long filaments.

Mountain laurels grow slowly and live a long time, eventually maturing at sizes of 8 to 12 feet high by 4 to 8 feet wide. Shrubs that receive some sun produce more flowers and develop rounder, fuller forms than those grown in dense shade. Aged plants can develop interesting, contorted trunks so plant mountain laurels where you can leave them alone instead of pruning to control size or shape. Mountain laurel grows in zones 4–9, so this shrub is slightly more tolerant of both heat and cold than rhododendrons are.

Shedding blossoms decorate the ground beneath mountain laurels, adding to their dainty beauty.

The distinctive flowers of the native mountain laurel seem to swarm over these shrubs from late May to June.

A SUBSTITUTE PLANT FOR DRY, ALKALINE SOIL

If your soil is dry and has a naturally high pH, you can't grow rhododendron or mountain laurel. However, you may be able to grow Texas mountain laurel, *Sophora secundiflora*. This southwestern native likes hot weather, rocky well-drained soil, sun, and open spaces. Plants form large, open shrubs or shrubby small trees, ranging in size from 6 to 15 feet high and occasionally 30 feet tall. Leaves remain shiny green year-round. Best of all, Texas mountain laurel produces large, drooping clusters of purple blossoms. My sister in Texas calls these "grape Kool-Aid trees" because that's what the flower fragrance reminds her of.

The deep taproot of Texas mountain laurel makes transplanting challenging. Many homeowners collect seeds to start in their landscapes. It is easier to coax green seeds into germination than the hard, red ripened seeds. The latter must be soaked and scraped with sandpaper for any hope of a seedling emerging. Texas mountain laurels grow slowly. Don't fertilize them to speed growth else flowering may be delayed. Once established, this is a plant that thrives on neglect. Avoid planting in wet or compacted soils, although rocky soil is fine. Do not overwater.

shrubs is a little like shopping for crepe myrtles; it is best to buy them in bloom so you can confirm the color you're getting. (Tags may be misleading or just plain wrong.)

To grow rhododendrons successfully, you must first determine the pH classification of your soil. You can purchase test kits or see your local extension service, but the easiest way to get a good idea of your soil's pH is to make note of indicator plants. If there are azaleas, dogwoods, blueberries, and other rhododendrons growing in your neighborhood, your soil is likely to be on the acidic end of the scale. Hydrangeas that regularly bloom blue instead of pink indicate the same thing. Acidic soils are perfect for growing rhododendrons. But if there's a noticeable lack of the plants mentioned above, it is probable that your soil has a high pH, making it alkaline (calcareous or limestone-based). Hydrangea flowers grown in alkaline soils naturally bloom pink instead of blue. If your soil is alkaline, forget about growing rhododendrons. (Aucuba is a shade-loving evergreen shrub that's far easier to keep happy in alkaline soil.)

Lucky homeowners with acidic soil, shade, and summers that are relatively mild when compared to blasting coastal heat are the ones who can plant rhododendrons in their landscapes. Moisture is important, too, especially during that first hot summer after planting. Keep roots cool and moist with generous amounts of mulch, but keep it several inches away from trunks. To water your rhodies, leave a trickling hose at the foot of each shrub in turn. Allow plants to dry out between watering—constantly wet roots will kill a rhododendron. Established plants require supplemental watering only during droughts.

Soil preparation is important when adding new rhododendrons to your landscape. These shrubs prefer fertile soil that's rich with organic matter. Mix plenty of compost, decayed leaves, peat, pine bark, or a combination of these at a ratio of two parts good stuff to one part native soil. Dig holes wider than they are deep so you've got plenty of room to add this delectable soil mixture. Set new plants in their holes so that the top of the rootball protrudes slightly higher than the adjacent, undisturbed soil.

Choose shady locations for rhododendrons. Partial shade is best because a dose of sunlight will keep plants full of foliage and flowers. All-day dappled shade or half-day shade is fine. In zone 7 and at higher elevations, rhododendrons are rarely damaged by afternoon sun if they have good soil and adequate moisture. In more southerly areas where rhododendrons may be marginal, plant these pretty shrubs in spots shielded from hot afternoon rays. Morning sun is fine. You can also grow rhododendrons in all-day shade if you don't mind plants that are more irregularly shaped with open forms and fewer flowers. Rhododendrons with foliage that yellows are in need of fertilizer. Look for some that includes rhododendrons on the label and apply per package directions (more is not better). Most rhododendron food includes magnesium sulfate, aluminum sulfate, or elemental sulfur to lower the soil pH, making it more acidic.

Trees

Showy Trees

Dogwood

The South is wrestling with a dogwood dilemma. This beloved tree, feted at festivals and mapped on viewing trails, has spent the last few decades succumbing to a range of problems. Dogwood anthracnose has caused cankers to appear on trunks, branches to wither, and entire colonies of trees to die. The less-than-lethal leafspot anthracnose has been discoloring foliage and thwarting flowering, while powdery mildew has been severely stunting growth and making surviving trees just plain ugly.

Should we abandon the species? Never again plant this little tree known for early-spring flowers that adorn bare branches like clouds of butterflies frozen in flight? I say no. Anthracnose, anshmacnose. The dogwood is too dainty, too pretty, too distinctive, and too useful to cross it off the landscaping list. Besides, what would all those towns with dogwood festivals do? North Carolina would have to select a new state tree and poor old Virginia would have to choose both a new state tree and state flower. That just wouldn't do.

The dogwood decline began in our region in the early 1980s among native populations of *Cornus florida*. Entire colonies were wiped out, and some nursery stock was infected, too. Western North Carolina was badly hit. Since then, botanists have learned more about diagnosing the dogwood's woes, and the prognosis isn't nearly as gloomy as it is rumored to be.

We can plant dogwoods in our landscapes. In fact, we should plant them to help repopulate the South with this lovely tree. Not only did we lose trees to disease, but the dogwood deficit also increased because trees that died naturally of old age weren't replaced during the planting lull that

GETTING ACQUAINTED

Deciduous small tree (bare in winter)

20 feet high by 20 feet wide; older trees may reach 30 feet or more

Showy white flowers in early spring before leaves; reliable autumn color shows up early

Slow rate of growth

High shade; needs some sun for flowering and health benefits; avoid all-day sun or hot western summer sun

Acidic, well-drained soil; not for alkaline soil or urban areas

Good choice for growing beneath tall trees, such as pines; attractive in the foreground as an accent or in the background as a pleasant surprise

Pairs well with periwinkle, bluestar, yellow archangel, liriope, mondo grass, Lenten rose, dead nettle, and daffodil

Zones 4–9

Our region has been losing its trademark dogwoods to anthracnose for years. But new information is helping keep these trees healthy, and a new fungal-resistant cultivar is putting dogwoods back into landscapes.

Trees: Showy

NAMED SELECTIONS

Studies have shown that the white-flowering Appalachian Spring® dogwood resists killer anthracnose. Plant it if you can find it for sale. It may be more readily available from Tennessee nurseries, as the tree's commercial release is handled there.

Other dogwoods in the Appalachian® series, including 'Karen's Blush', 'Jean's Snow', and 'Kay's Mist', are marketed as resistant to powdery mildew. The 'Karen's Blush' selection has white petals tinged with pink, while the other two are white.

A cross between the flowering dogwood and the kousa has resulted in a group of dogwoods known as Rutgers Hybrids. These include the selections 'Ruth Ellen', 'Celestial', 'Aurora', and 'Constellation', which have exhibited fewer problems with nonlethal leafspot and powdery mildew in field trials.

MORNING VERSUS AFTERNOON SUN

Keep in mind that the farther north you live, the more sun your dogwoods can take and the more sun you should allow them. The farther south you live, the more your dogwood should be shaded from blistering afternoon sun, particularly during summer. Morning sun is beneficial for dogwoods throughout the South.

WHITE VERSUS PINK

Purists plant only white-flowering dogwoods, and I admit to once succumbing to the elitist appeal of this camp. But while photographing a breath-taking pink dogwood in bloom, I realized, "What's not to like?"

As to which is tougher, the answer depends on whom you ask. Some studies indicate that pink-flowering dogwoods are more susceptible to deadly dogwood anthracnose while others show that white-flowering dogwoods, especially those grown in all-day sun, are more likely to come down with the ugly-but-survivable leafspot anthracnose. At present, the only *Cornus florida* dogwood that experts agree is truly resistant to fungal disease is Appalachian Spring®, a white-blooming tree.

TOUGH LOVE

While it is a good idea to improve soil drainage by adding sand or gypsum to the planting hole for a dogwood, avoid the temptation to mix in a lot of lushly decomposing organic matter. Studies have shown that dogwoods grown in poor, dry soil actually withstand disease better than those grown in rich soil. You'll have to water a little more to get your tree started and later during droughts—dogwoods have shallow roots—but you'll help it adapt for the long run.

KOUSA DOGWOODS

Botanists recommend the disease-resistant kousa dogwood (*Cornus kousa*) as a substitute for *C. florida* dogwoods. The kousa dogwood grows in full sun. Although this late-blooming tree is a great addition to sunny spots in the landscape, it is not a true replacement for the native dogwood that brightens the shadows with early-spring blossoms.

followed the anthracnose troubles. Horticultural studies have shown us that how and where we plant dogwoods has a lot to do with keeping these valuable trees healthy.

First, the whys of planting. Dogwoods are traditional heralds of spring. Their large, flat "flowers" appear early, when the trees are otherwise still naked. Native dogwoods bloom snowy white, but selections bred to bloom pink are for sale, too. Dogwoods thrive in semi-shade, making them a natural understory tree in Southern woodlands. Trees stay small, just 20 feet high and wide, and summer foliage shows off the trees' graceful form. Dogwood leaves are among the first to turn in the autumn, in shades of orange, red, and burgundy. Berries ripen to a bright, glossy red in autumn and will persist on slender branches into winter unless devoured by birds and squirrels first. The dogwood is a good little tree, one well worth growing.

But no one wants to plant a tree that's not going to thrive. So take steps toward success. First, buy dogwoods only from a reputable nursery. Never dig plants from the woods or buy trees that have been collected instead of propagated. You don't want to import a problem into your landscape. If you can find them for sale, Appalachian Spring® dogwoods are the best choice. *Cornus florida* Appalachian Spring® was thoroughly tested by the Tennessee Agricultural Extension Service at the University of Tennessee and found to be anthracnose resistant. All Appalachian Spring® dogwoods are grafts resulting from a single, naturally occurring survivor tree.

Next, carefully choose the locations for any dogwoods you add to your landscape. With trees growing wild in the woods, common wisdom holds that dogwoods prefer plenty of shade. While dense shade does keep trees from becoming dry and stressed by heat, it also creates problems. When it rains, foliage dries more slowly in shade. This is a big contributor to the spread of the lethal dogwood anthracnose—this killer's spores are spread by water. Increased humidity in shade also promotes the development of powdery mildew.

A

B

C

D

E

So if shade is problematic yet sunny spots get too hot, what's a gardener to do? The answer is to seek areas with a condition known as high shade. Just like it sounds, high shade occurs in the shadows cast by tall trees. Mature pines are great for creating high shade. The canopy of these tall trees blocks hot damaging sunrays without trapping humidity under a low layer of leaves. High shade promotes good air circulation, which allows dogwood leaves to dry quickly and helps prevent powdery mildew. High shade also means that the shade isn't total—sun can slant under the tall canopies for part of the day, which also helps keep dogwood foliage dry. It also increases photosynthetic activity, making the tree manufacture more food, which helps it stay healthy and able to withstand disease. A good dose of sunshine promotes flowering as well. So dogwoods that receive some sun are more likely to remain healthy and also produce showier,

(A) Nearby mature oaks and pines provide high shade, the ideal light condition for dogwoods. Studies have shown that dogwoods receiving some sunlight are more disease-resistant than those grown in all-day shade. However, hot afternoon sun is damaging to dogwoods.

(B) Dogwoods that receive some sun have brighter autumn color.

(C) Dogwoods are one of the first trees to welcome autumn to the landscape.

(D) Pointy red berries grow in clusters. Unless eaten by squirrels or wild birds, the dogwood's fruit will remain shiny red on gray branches through winter

(E) The true flower is the green part in the center. The dogwood flower is surrounded by showy white bracts that are actually leaves, not petals.

more profuse crops of blossoms each spring than dogwoods grown in dense, all-day shade.

Don't mimic the natural habitat of wild dogwoods. Instead, plant your nursery-bought dogwoods where each can stand alone. It is imperative that you avoid squashing dogwoods up against other plants, walls, fences, or houses. If you plant multiple trees, separate them with other plants in between. Never let your dogwoods touch one another; if one is infected, another kind of tree between dogwoods may be able to avoid spread of disease.

The best time to plant dogwoods varies by area. Figure out what the rainy season is in your area, and make sure to avoid planting any dogwoods then. Instead, plant new dogwoods in the opposite season, giving young trees a chance to settle into their new home before monsoons arrive. The reason is that recently planted trees are weaker than established ones, and so it is harder for new transplants to fight off infections that are more likely to plague dogwoods during wet weather. Planting during the dry season—and dutifully watering roots regularly with a hose—gives young dogwoods a fighting chance if anthracnose visits the neighborhood later when weather is wet.

A few simple rules will help keep trees healthy. Always keep dogwood foliage as dry as humanly possible by never spraying them with a hose or sprinkler. Reposition irrigation nozzles to prevent water spray from hitting dogwoods. However, keep in mind that trees weakened by drought are more susceptible to problems when rains return, so provide all dogwoods, large and small, with supplemental water during extra-dry conditions. The way to water your dogwood is to leave a slow-running hose on top of the ground not far from the trunk. Allow water to seep into the ground without wetting the foliage or trunk. But don't overdo it; too much water is as bad as too little. In the heat of summer, roots of dogwoods that are less than a year old should be watered every other day. During drought conditions, water older trees every seven to ten days by giving roots a good soaking with the hose.

Dogwoods have delicate bark, so you must avoid damaging trunks with landscape equipment. Trunk wounds are prime entry points for pests and diseases. Surround each dogwood trunk with a 3-inch layer of organic mulch, but apply it like a donut with the trunk in the hole. (Keep mulch 12 inches from the trunk.) As the tree's spread widens, increase the mulch to carpet the area beneath the dogwood's canopy. Mulch helps keep the soil cool and moist and also suppresses growth of grass and weeds. This, in turn, prevents the need to use string trimmers and mowers in the vicinity of the trunk, reducing chances of damage. Pull any persistent weeds by hand. It is fine to let groundcover grow into the mulched area.

In autumn, rake away fallen dogwoods leaves and dispose of them off your property. To avoid spreading damaging spores or windblown fungal problems, do not compost dogwood leaves. Don't forget to occasionally water dogwood roots during a dry winter. Remove any soft shoots growing

F

I

G

H

from roots or low on trunks in late autumn; sterilize pruning tools with rubbing alcohol before and after use. Cut away withered, stunted, or dead branches any time of year—as soon as you notice the problem—taking care to sterilize pruning tools. Destroy or dispose of such cuttings off-site.

None of this is as tricky as it sounds. Buying a healthy plant and choosing the correct location is half the battle. A little attention to dogwoods during droughts, a few basic rules about pruning and raking, keeping sprinklers away from foliage—none of these tasks is particularly taxing. Chemical control of major infections is more challenging and should be pursued only under the direction of a knowledgeable county extension agent familiar with dogwood diseases. But with dogwoods planted in the right locations, and a little luck, you may not ever have a problem in your garden at all. Though many dogwoods in the South were lost or damaged, there are still enough healthy, lovely trees to prove that dogwoods can survive and thrive in the home landscape.

(F) and (G) Pink-flowering dogwoods add a beauty all their own to warm spring days.
(H) 'Bay Beauty' is a double-flowering selection that shows promise in resisting fungal infections and powdery mildew. Good heat tolerance makes this tree a good choice for lower zone 8 and zone 9.
(I) Even trees grown in shaded locations turn muted shades of red and orange in autumn.

Acer palmatum

Japanese Maple

You don't have to grow a Japanese-themed garden to find a home for a Japanese maple in your landscape. These little trees are among the most elegant of plants.

Japanese maple is one of those plants that prompts sighs. Whether they're sighs of bliss or envy depends on whether you've got one in your landscape. Japanese maples are extremely graceful shade-lovers, grown for their form and foliage, not for their unnoticeable flowers. There are more choices of Japanese maples than there are kinds of ice cream, so picking one is a matter of suiting your taste and available space. Some plants make mounding shrubs, others are dainty miniature trees, and still others grow to become good-sized trees comparable to mature dogwoods. Summer leaf colors range from bright green to olive to purplish red. In autumn the choices include leaves that turn bright yellow, orange, burgundy, and nearly glow-in-the-dark red.

No matter what color they are, the leaves of all Japanese maples are palmate, meaning the lobes of the each leaf are arranged like fingers attached to the palm of a hand. Some selections of Japanese maples have pointy, starry leaves; others have finely cut, lacy foliage; and still others have leaves so delicate that they're classified as threadleaf. Even the largest-leaved Japanese maples are fine in texture. This means that glancing at any Japanese maple gathers an impression of multitudes of separate leaves instead of just a solid blob of greenery. The lacier selections add a touch of almost unbelievable delicacy to the landscape.

Blistering sun and endless heat are bad for these plants, but we Southerners can grow Japanese maples successfully by compensating for our hot summers with shade. The hotter your area's summer temperatures, the more shade and water you'll need to provide to keep Japanese maple happy. With the exception of frost-free areas where the sun is too

A

B

C

D

(A) If autumn color is your goal, make sure your Japanese maple gets at least four hours of sunlight every day, but protect it scorching afternoon rays. Usually, Japanese maples that are green in summer have more dramatic autumn color than those with colored summer foliage.

(B) Which autumn hue you end up with depends on which selection you purchase. Talk to nursery staff and read plant tags, as there are hundreds of different kinds of Japanese maples.

(C) Twisting, irregular trunks add to the Japanese maple's charm. Expect to pay more for specimens as picturesque as this one.

(D) Growing a fine-leaved Japanese maple beside any coarse texture, such as a smooth stone, will give your landscape a professionally designed look.

E

F

G

H

I

(E) Small stature and slow growth makes Japanese maples ideal for courtyards.

(F) Trunks of larger selections become muscular with age and keep Japanese maples attractive after leaves drop.

(G) The fine-textured foliage of laceleaf and threadleaf varieties shows off beautifully beside water.

(H) Some kinds of Japanese maples get larger than others, but they all grow slowly. This tree is over twenty years old. You may want to splurge on a good-sized Japanese maple for your landscape.

(I) Head-turning autumn foliage ranges from fiery yellows, oranges, and reds to deep burgundy, depending on the named selection you choose.

J   K

strong, Japanese maples grown throughout the South are fine in morning sun. Afternoon sun is damaging for these trees in all but the coolest of
Southern gardens. Trees grown at higher elevations can take sun most of
the day, as can Japanese maples grown in areas where temperature spikes
into the nineties are news, not the norm. Unfortunately, if you live in an
area that regularly sees back-to-back days of triple-digit heat, rarely or
never receives frost, or has very alkaline soils (limestone based), your sighs
will be limited to those of envy. The outlook for growing a Japanese maple
under such conditions is quite poor. Likewise, windy settings that dry
these trees are not conducive to good growth.

But in the right situations, Japanese maples are quite tough. They don't
mind crowded roots, making them ideal for courtyards and patios. Such
settings are good for admiring these dainty trees up close. You can even
grow them for years in large containers. Be aware that Japanese maples
grown near heat-reflecting paving require additional water.

The sight of a Japanese maple beside a pond, stream, or waterfall in
your landscape automatically qualifies you for bragging rights. The graceful form of any selection of this plant shows off beautifully beside water.
Make sure plants grown close to water features have good drainage.
Although Japanese maples need regular watering to help them beat the
heat, they can't stand wet roots. So unless you're blessed with rich soil
that naturally drains well, mix plenty of sand, peat, and large-particle
organic matter into damp soil.

Never bump Japanese maple trunks with mowers, shovels, or string
trimmers. Mulch beneath young trees but keep mulch a few inches away
from trunks. When watering, apply a trickling stream of water to the
root area, allowing it to soak slowly into the ground. This encourages
deeper root growth and increases tolerance to heat and dryness. Mid to
late autumn is the best time to plant a Japanese maple, giving it ample
opportunity to get fresh roots growing before the long, hot days arrive.
Fortunately, these slow-growing trees transplant well at larger sizes, so
you can buy a big one if impatience controls your wallet.

(J) The flowers of Japanese maples are delicately
shy—you'll have to look closely to see them.
(K) Like all maples, the Japanese species produce
seeds as winged samaras.

Aesculus pavia

Also sold as *Aesculus splendens*

Red Buckeye

GETTING ACQUAINTED

Deciduous tree (bare in winter)

6 to 20 feet high by 8 to 20 feet wide; form
is often charmingly irregular and shrubby
when grown in shade

Big red blooms brighten deep shadows in mid
to late spring

Moderate growth rate

Native

All-day shade, partial shade

Damp, woodsy soil

Good choice for dry shade, moist shade,
wooded lots, natural areas, and creek banks

Pairs well with foamflower, trillium, astilbe,
bleeding hearts, yellow archangel, Virginia
bluebell, Solomon's seal, Virginia sweetspire,
fothergilla, hydrangeas, star magnolia, periwinkle, pieris, and celandine poppy

Zones 4–8

Red buckeyes are a good excuse to let fallen
leaves decay naturally instead of hauling them
away. These small trees prefer soil enriched by leaf
humus. Add compost (homemade or bagged) to
planting holes to encourage root growth in new
trees. Water freshly planted trees regularly during
the first hot season.

The most difficult thing about growing red buckeyes is finding them for sale. Though they grow wild in many areas, these small trees aren't common nursery stock, so a native plant sale hosted by a specialty plant nursery, botanical garden, or garden club may be your best bet.

Red buckeyes prefer shade and enough moisture to get them growing. If these two conditions are met, then you're all set. It doesn't matter

if your soil is acidic or alkaline, as long as it isn't compacted. Established plants will grow happily in dry shade, one of the most difficult conditions for growing good-sized ornamental plants. Newly planted red buckeyes need to be watered during their first hot season, but after that, trees grown in shade can thrive unattended. Red buckeyes will also grow in damp soil, where they'll spread to form patches of attractive, shrubby trees. Colonies form in dry soil, too, but not as rapidly.

You can grow red buckeyes in sun, where they'll become taller and more treelike than shade-grown buckeyes, but trees in the sun may require supplemental watering during dry spells. All red buckeyes should be positioned where they're protected from hot afternoon sun in all but the coolest of gardens of the South. For carefree landscaping, plant red buckeyes in the shade beneath other, taller trees to add a lower layer of foliage, known as the understory. Soil rich with decomposing leaves is ideal, making red buckeyes good for woodsy spots in landscapes, where they'll grow into mounded shapes.

There's more to recommend this tree besides ease of cultivation. Red buckeye's foliage is coarse-textured (design-speak for large leaves), so it

A

B

shows up well from a distance. Long droopy leaflets grow along stems in sets of five to seven. New growth is coppery when it first unfurls in spring. Showy red flowers appear in mid to late spring, held aloft like candles. Though red tends to fade into the shadows—that is, in comparison with white or yellow, which gleam in the shade—the contrast between the red buckeye's ruby flowers and green foliage is quite eye-catching. Both humans and hummingbirds find the red blooms attractive.

In autumn, husks open to reveal shiny brown nutlike fruits; these are the buckeyes of the plant's name. A buckeye is said to bring good luck when someone finds one and gives it to you. Foliage turns yellow before dropping. Bare branches are gray in winter.

C

(A) Left alone in the shade, red buckeyes spread to form small, attractive colonies of little trees and shrubby siblings.
(B) The new growth of red buckeye is tinged with bronze, and flower buds are pale green in early spring.
(C) The foliage of red buckeye becomes glossy green by summer.

Cercis canadensis

Also sold as eastern redbud, Judas tree

GETTING ACQUAINTED

Deciduous tree (bare in winter)

20 to 25 feet high by 15 to 20 wide

Purple to pink flowers cover branches in early
   spring before leaves appear

Rapid rate of growth

Native

Partial shade; morning or afternoon sun is fine

Any well-drained soil

Good choice for wooded lots, growing beneath
   larger trees, or beside patios, decks, parking
   areas, in courtyards, as street trees, or in
   niches formed by architecture

Pairs well with Japanese kerria, rhododendron,
   beautyberry, Japanese painted fern, Lenten
   rose, daffodil, liriope, mondo grass, star
   magnolia, Spanish bluebell, yellow archangel, periwinkle, oakleaf hydrangea, windflower, and hosta

Zones 4–9

Spring fever hits redbud early. Flowers appear
before leaves.

Redbud

Redbud's early spring flowers aren't red—they're more of a purple-pink, really—but they do resemble buds. Blossoms open in stemless clusters clinging to twigs and older branches. This odd flowering habit makes trees seem as if they're coated with color when in bloom. Redbuds are modest members of the landscape for most of the year, but they steal the show during the waning days of winter. That's when flowers appear—a welcome flush of color when most surrounding landscapes are still bare and gray.

Although you can grow redbud in the sun, this little tree is a useful choice for shade. It grows wild as an understory tree, meaning it naturally fills in beneath pines, oaks, hickories, and maples. Unlike some hard-to-

find native trees, redbud is readily available in most nurseries and garden centers. This species grows quickly, so you can start off with an inexpensive little plant and enjoy a small tree just a few years later. Redbuds don't last for generations, so they're not the best choice for planting in someone's honor. However, a redbud's life expectancy is a good fifteen to twenty years, and that's pretty much carefree.

Redbuds are tough. These trees are drought tolerant and don't require fertilizing or coddling to get growing. They aren't picky about soil, growing equally well in acidic soils (where azaleas thrive) and in alkaline soils (where azaleas won't grow). In fact, redbuds will put up with just about anything except standing water. You can crowd them under larger trees, and redbuds will adapt nicely. They're great for planting along the edges of woods to dress up views. Redbuds are equally at home in formal gardens and naturalized beds, and beside parking areas, walkways, benches, or patios.

A

B

C

D

REDBUD

(A) Harsh winters rarely deter redbud's early-spring flowering, and blossoms keep their color through most late cold snaps.

(B) Flat seedpods persist on redbud trees through autumn and winter and provide food for wildlife.

(C) Heart-shaped leaves are easy to identify, making redbud a favorite choice for school leaf-collection projects. Foliage turns yellow in autumn before falling.

(D) The summer canopies of redbud are thick and lush.

WHY THEY GROW WILD

Including redbud in your landscape will yield one chore: Plan on uprooting unwanted seedlings that result from seedpods spread by wind and birds. Fortunately, the sprouts are easy to transplant, so you can move them elsewhere in your garden or give them away to friends and neighbors if you like. Unless a tree is very old, large, and prolific, a redbud will usually yield fewer unwanted seedlings than a large oak tree does when fallen acorns sprout each spring.

NAMED SELECTIONS

'ALBA' AND 'ROYAL WHITE': white flowers

'FOREST PANSY': leaves emerge dark purple in spring, fade to green in summer; flowers are purplish

'Forest Pansy'

COVEY®: weeping form

'TENNESSEE PINK': pink flowers

TEXAS REDBUD (Cercis canadensis var. texensis): thick leaves are quite heat tolerant; thrives in alkaline soil

Star Magnolia

Magnolia stellata

Also sold as *Magnolia kobus* var. *stellata*

Not all magnolias are huge, yard-eating mammoths. Here's one that's a delicate little thing. Star magnolia is named for the stellar white flowers it produces in early spring. Though these trees grow slowly and stay shrubby for the first years of their lives, star magnolias will bloom even when they're merely sapling-sized. Trees produce more branches and more flowers as plants mature. Use these pretty plants to dress up the edges of woodlands or scatter them throughout large shady beds. You can also plant a single star magnolia as an accent tree.

Star magnolia is deciduous, so it is bare all winter. However, noticeably large and fuzzy buds form on twig tips, persisting through the cold

months and reminding us that spring will come again. Snow and ice do not harm the buds. You'll be glad leaves are down when those early blossoms adorn the bare, gray branches. Without foliage, the white flowers show off even more. Buds don't open all at once, allowing you to enjoy flowers for several weeks. Blooms appear early, from late winter to the dawn of spring. Though a freeze can turn opened flowers brown, the trees themselves are cold hardy and won't be damaged. In freeze-prone areas, the best way to avoid losing crops of blossoms is to plant star magnolias *away* from the southern exposure in your landscape. This will prevent flowers from opening too soon and getting zapped by frost.

Star magnolias thrive in the shade but require sun to bloom. That's not as tricky as it sounds, considering the early arrival of flowers. Blooms open long before oaks and other hardwoods sport leaves—winter sun can easily reach star magnolias planted in the shade of such larger trees. The more sun a star magnolia receives, the better it blooms, though trees grown in full sun will require water during droughts. The farther south you live, the more important it becomes to plant star magnolias where they won't get fried by western rays of afternoon sun. It is the blazing rays that are dam-

Star magnolias may bloom before spring fever has lured you out into the garden, so choose planting locations you can enjoy from inside your home.

aging, not the heat. Star magnolia is a reliable plant in all but the south-ernmost third of Florida.

Star magnolias don't care about soil pH, so homeowners in limestone-based alkaline areas can grow them as well as gardeners with acidic soil. These tough little trees prefer fertile, well-drained soil, but will grow in less-than-ideal conditions and even tolerate wet soil. Star magnolias grow slowly and stay shrubby for several years before becoming more treelike with age. Trees may have single or multiple trunks and charming, crooked branches. Canopies become mounded and spreading as the trees mature.

When selecting a site for a star magnolia in your landscape, plan ahead for the tree's eventual spreading shape. Mature star magnolias are wide with low branches and may crowd sidewalks or parking areas, so give them room to grow. Lower branches can be removed to train a star magnolia into a more traditional tree shape, but it is best to do this when branches are young and thin. Whacking away at thick, woody branches will ruin the form of a mature tree.

STAR MAGNOLIA

(A) Star magnolias don't require pruning. If you cut them back, you'll remove the buds for next spring's flowers.

(B) Though autumn is the best planting time for most trees, star magnolias are better off planted during the wettest part of spring, after the danger of frost has passed. Fuzzy buds are showy on bare branches in winter.

(C) The floppy white flowers of star magnolia bear a sweet scent in early spring. Petals elongate as flowers mature.

(D) If given space, sunlight, and time, star magnolias can grow larger than most dogwoods. Trees grown in the shade make pretty little shrubby trees.

NAMED SELECTIONS

'Centennial': blush-pink flowers fade to white; very heat and cold tolerant

'Royal Star': white flowers, extra petals; later blooming decreases chances of cold damage

'Jane Platt': flowers are rich pink when first opened, turning paler with age; good heat tolerance

Trees for Privacy

Eastern Hemlock

Tsuga canadensis

Also sold as Canadian hemlock, eastern Canadian hemlock

We Southerners like snow. That's because we don't have to live with it on a regular basis. Claiming lack of experience, we can't drive in the stuff—and if we could, we'd pretend we couldn't—so that each rare snowfall becomes a holiday. This makes it fun to buy into the romantic image of snow, dreaming of elusive white Christmases and sleigh bells ringing. No tree transports a Southerner to the land of Courier and Ives winter scenery like the sight of a snow-covered eastern hemlock.

Of course, snow isn't essential to enjoy an eastern hemlock, but a good dusting does bring out this tree's finer points: the classic pyramidal form and the feathery branches that stay green year-round. You'll find eastern hemlocks growing in cooler parts of the South, such as the mountainous areas of Tennessee, Georgia, and Alabama, the woodsy areas of Virginia and Kentucky, and the chillier parts of inland North Carolina. All of these spots may experience hot summers, but they aren't likely to see weeks on end of temperatures in the high nineties. Hemlock lives where triple-digit thermometer readings are big news. If you live where long hot spells with no rainfall are more common, see "Hemlock Substitutes" on page 118.

If you can grow eastern hemlock in your landscape, you'll know it, because everyone around you will be growing this graceful evergreen tree, too. Young trees thrive in full to partial shade, so you can easily add them to a wooded lot. To grow an eastern hemlock that features weeping branches and takes on a mounded shape in maturity, look for the selections 'Pendula' or 'Sargentii'. Decomposed fallen leaves create the ideal soil condition for hemlocks, making these trees a good choice for natural areas where

GETTING ACQUAINTED

Evergreen tree

40 to 80 feet high by 25 to 40 feet wide

Feathery needle foliage stays green year-round; produces tiny brown cones

Moderate rate of growth

Does not tolerate drought, extended extreme heat, or pollution

All-day shade, partial shade, or full sun

Rich, woodsy soil that's well drained; not for wet or alkaline soil

Good choice for screening views, adding privacy, growing on wooded lots; thrives in the mountains

Pairs well with flowering shrubs; grow behind Japanese kerria, rhododendron, fothergilla, hydrangeas, beautyberry, Virginia sweetspire, gooseneck loosestrife, and Pinxterbloom azalea; groundcovers include yellow archangel, littleleaf periwinkle, and dead nettle; daffodil

Zones 3–7

Eastern hemlocks are shaped like Christmas trees. It's not uncommon for lower branches to rest on the ground. Plant these trees where they can enlarge in circumference, and don't remove the lower limbs.

Trees: Privacy

DON'T HACK YOUR HEMLOCK

Though foliage of young hemlocks can be trimmed regularly to form hedges, hemlocks grown as trees are better left unpruned. Think long and hard before removing the woody bottom branches of an eastern hemlock. All this does is reveal a circle of dry, barren earth where brown needles collect. No matter how many lower branches you chop off, you're not going to be able to grow much of anything beneath the canopy because the tree's feeder roots absorb all available moisture and nutrients. Once you've cut those branches, they'll never grow back. Instead of enjoying a graceful sweep of greenery, you'll view stubs on a trunk. And remember, if you hack off branches, anything that was screened by the lower boughs will be revealed. So think of your eastern hemlock as a tree wearing a floor-length gown: Don't mess with the hemline.

HEMLOCK SUBSTITUTES

DEODAR CEDAR, *Cedrus deodara*

If you live in an area where azaleas and dogwoods won't grow without being pampered, a deodar cedar is a better choice for your landscape than an eastern hemlock. Deodars thrive in alkaline soil, whereas hemlocks don't. Though the branches aren't quite as feathery and full, deodar cedar is about as northern-looking a tree as you can get in the rare-frost and frost-free parts of the South. This was my cheater tree in Orlando, Florida, when I was charged with creating a planting scheme to complement a Cape Cod style hotel at Disney World. I included deodar cedars in the design, relying on their evergreen needles and pyramidal forms to evoke a cold-weather climate. This trick worked because the trees themselves are quite heat tolerant. Deodar cedars grow from zone 7 to zone 9. Plant this tree in well-drained soil in full sun or partial shade. Regular watering is recommended for the first few years.

CAROLINA HEMLOCK, *Tsuga caroliniana*

This close relative of the eastern hemlock is native to Appalachia. Slightly smaller, stiffer, and slower growing, the Carolina hemlock tolerates heat a little better than the eastern hemlock, though it still isn't a good choice for downtown conditions. Of the two, you're more likely to find an eastern hemlock for sale at a nursery.

A

B

C

D

TREES: PRIVACY

E

you don't plan to rake. If you don't have such a rake-free zone in your landscape, use your desire to grow eastern hemlocks as an excuse to create one. You can dump fallen leaves raked from elsewhere beneath hemlocks.

These evergreens are so well suited for wooded areas that only newly planted trees require watering to get them going. After that, you can pretty much neglect eastern hemlocks and just watch them grow. Trees grow upward of 80 feet, usually finding sunshine along the way. Tolerance to sun and drought increases with maturity. The more sun a young tree receives, the more watering you'll need to do during any hot, dry spells of its early years. It is not essential to plant eastern hemlocks in shade, but it is easier.

Because these evergreen trees shed needles a little at a time throughout the year instead of going bare in winter, hemlocks are excellent for year-round screening. Plant them to block unwanted views (think propane tanks or roadways) and to add privacy to your home and yard. A row or grove of hemlocks planted 10 to 15 feet apart will grow to form a green wall with multiple peaks. A single eastern hemlock should be planted where it can stand alone for optimum admiration; such placement will make your hemlock a specimen tree. Avoid planting hemlocks too close to houses, walkways, or parking areas, as the bottom circle of branches widens considerably with age. Limbs are much too low to walk beneath, so plan accordingly. Plant shrubs and perennials where they can be viewed with eastern hemlock in the background; don't plant them within eventual reach of the tree's branches.

(A) Eastern hemlocks bring out the best of occasional snowfalls.
(B) Budding green cones form on eastern hemlock in summer.
(C) By winter, the little cones open and dangle downward.
(D) Evergreen foliage keeps eastern hemlocks fresh in all seasons.
(E) Young eastern hemlocks planted in a shaded natural area will eventually form a carefree screen that's thick and tall.

Groundcovers

Lamium maculatum

Also sold as spotted dead nettle, lamium

Dead Nettle

GETTING ACQUAINTED

Evergreen groundcover

6 inches tall; spreading

Green or variegated foliage; white, pink, or
purple flowers in spring

Moderate to rapid rate of growth

Good drought tolerance in shady conditions

Partial shade to mostly shady; protect from hot
afternoon sun in zones 8 and 9; established
plants tolerate dry shade near tree roots

Any soil that's not wet or very compacted;
moist soil is fine

Good choice for shady rock gardens, filling
empty spaces in planting beds, and growing
in containers, planters, and window boxes;
plant near entries, patios, walkways, entries,
benches, and garden sculpture

Pairs well with bluestar, daffodil, dogwood,
impatiens, caladium, liriope, mondo grass,
star magnolia, fothergilla, Japanese kerria,
Japanese maple, beautyberry, leatherleaf
mahonia, hosta, eastern hemlock, hydrangeas, Japanese painted fern, Spanish bluebell, and holly fern

Zones 3–9

Stinging nettles are painful plants and therefore, someone thought it would be a good idea to distinguish between the nettles that can hurt you and the ones that can't. Unfortunately, the plant-naming maestros overlooked self-explanatory options, such as "nice nettle" or "no-sting nettle," and settled on "dead nettle" instead. I always feel a little odd recommending a plant that sounds doomed, but rest assured, dead nettle is not easily killed. In fact, it belongs to the vigorous mint family, though its manners are an improvement over those of pushy culinary mints.

Dead nettle is valuable for its creeping habit of growth. Plants stay low; *Lamium maculatum* is usually only about 6 inches high. Each plant can

spread 2 to 3 feet in all directions from its crown, which is the point at which stems emerge above the soil surface from roots below. Each set of roots produces stems with a potential 3-foot spread, which can root themselves and spread 3 feet from that point and so on. That's why dead nettle is in the ground-cover category. Plants expand most rapidly in partially shaded situations when grown in fertile soil with even moisture. But once established, dead nettle will also grow in dry soil though at a more leisurely pace. Given ideal conditions, you may end up with more dead nettle than you bargained for, so make sure you want it before you plant it. But aggressive growth is less of a concern in the South than it is in cooler regions, as our summer heat seems to check dead nettle's enthusiasm somewhat. If plants become drooping and overheated, water them just enough to keep them going. They'll perk up again when temperatures drop.

Dead nettle has decorative foliage. Named selections offer a range of leaf schemes that combine green, white, gold, and silver in artful ways. The plants bloom, too, with their clustered flowers appearing in late spring

Dead nettle spreads to cover patches of bare
ground with decorative foliage that lasts year-
round. Flowers appear in late spring or early summer. Moist soil is good and dry soil is okay, while
wet soil is the worst for growing dead nettle.

This groundcover is a good choice for including in shaded window boxes, planters, hanging baskets, and containers. The scalloped leaves of the White and Pewter series are outlined in green. Dead nettle pairs well with impatiens.

or early summer. Blossom colors include white, light pink, rose pink, pinkish purple, and lavender. Both the foliage and the flowers of dead nettle are appealing. This plant ought to be planted in partially shaded pots, planters, hanging baskets, and window boxes far more often than it currently is. Stems tumble over the edges of containers, spilling this plant's charms into view. Dead nettle is durable enough for confined root conditions, though it will require a little more water in a pot than it does in the ground.

This groundcover grows in sun in northern gardens, but it prefers a bit of shade in the South. Grow dead nettle in all-day dappled shade or a spot that's sunny in the morning and shady in the afternoon. It will also grow in all-day shade, but flowering and spreading vigor will be reduced. In zone 7 and cooler areas, dead nettle can tolerate some afternoon sun, given fertile soil and occasional supplemental watering during heat waves. New plants need regular water to get them going. Taper off watering when you notice new growth. Dead nettle gets tougher as its roots spread, making it a candidate for those difficult spots in dry shade near tree roots. Add young plants to your landscape in spring or autumn by planting in beds of turned, softened soil that's amended with organic matter.

NAMED SELECTIONS

These colorful cultivars are improvements on the plainer *Lamium maculatum*, which is native to parts of the United States.

'ANNE GREENAWAY': golden leaves with green centers striped with silver; pink flowers

'AUREUM': light yellow leaves striped with white; pale pink flowers

'BEACON SILVER': silver leaves edged with green; deep lavender flowers

'BEEDHAM'S WHITE': golden leaves striped with white; white flowers

'CANNON'S GOLD': solid gold foliage; pink flowers

'CHEQUERS': green leaves striped with silver; deep pink flowers; vigorous grower

'GOLDEN ANNIVERSARY': green leaves striped with silver and edged heavily with gold; pink flowers

'ORCHID FROST': silver leaves edged in green; pinkish purple flowers

'PINK PEWTER': silver gray leaves edged with green; pink flowers

'PURPLE DRAGON': silver leaves edged in green; purple flowers

'RED NANCY': silver leaves edged with green; rose-pink flowers

'SHELL PINK': green leaves striped with silver; shell-pink flowers

'WHITE NANCY': silver leaves edged with green; white flowers; protect from sun

Liriope

Liriope muscari

Also sold as monkey grass, blue lily turf
Not to be confused with mondo grass
(*Ophiopogon japonicus*), which has dark
green narrow foliage and thrives in
shade

GETTING ACQUAINTED

Evergreen groundcover

12 to 18 inches high and wide

Clumps of arching foliage like wide green
    linguine remain year-round; purple
    flowers in summer

Rapid rate of growth

Tolerates drought

Resistant to insects and disease

Mostly shady to all-day sun

Any soil that's not wet

Good choice for narrow spaces, edging beds,
    filling empty areas, planting near patios,
    walkways, driveways, and pool decks; grow
    in parking areas, in front of taller plants, and
    as mass plantings

Pairs well with everything except bog plants

Zones 6–10

The light purple flowers of liriope grow on stalks
above foliage. This groundcover is also called
monkey grass.

Liriope and mondo grass are sometimes considered to be the same plant, but they're not. Though both are easy-to-grow clumping groundcovers, liriope is larger and lighter green and has wider blades. It also tolerates more sun than dark green mondo grass does. You'll enjoy the lavender flowers of liriope, whereas you can hardly see mondo's blossoms hidden among its foliage. Both groundcovers are evergreen, but of the two, liriope looks a little rattier in winter.

You can grow liriope in shade or sun, so there's no reason to protect it from hot western rays. It tolerates the reflected heat of paving better than mondo grass (*Ophiopogon japonicus*). You can grow liriope in a parking area or beside a sunny pool deck—it's that tough. Green liriope goes well with all color schemes and fits in everywhere. Grow it in front of shrubs or beneath trees for a fluffy effect that won't distract attention from fancier plants. Liriope is particularly useful in beds that are sometimes sunny and sometimes shady. Variegated liriope is an accent plant, and it must be placed with care to avoid visual competition with other showy members of the landscape.

Plant liriope in any soil that's not consistently damp. Established plants are drought tolerant and tough as nails. The arching clumps of foliage thicken and spread with age. You can leave them alone or dig them up and separate the roots to get new plants. Divide liriope any time of the year. Water young transplants regularly until new shoots appear. After that, plants can thrive on their own. It is not necessary to mow liriope, but you can if you want to remove last year's foliage. All mowing should be completed in late winter. If you wait until spring, you'll cut off the tips of new shoots, leaving your groundcover browned on the ends for the remainder of the growing season.

A

B

C

D

E

(A) A wide sweep of liriope makes a more attractive border than a single row outlining a bed.

(B) An ample foreground of liriope gives beds a finished look. Small, ornamental trees grown in liriope instead of grass will not be damaged by the use of mowers or string trimmers near their trunks.

(C) Flowers become glossy black berries that spill over by winter.

(D) Liriope is extremely useful for filling bare spots in shade where grass won't grow. Because this groundcover also takes sun, there's no concern about rays that reach the area.

(E) Liriope works equally well in symmetrically balanced formal landscapes and in more casual designs. This versatile plant grows in shade or sun.

NAMED SELECTIONS

'VARIEGATA': yellow and green striped foliage; purple flowers; use sparingly

'MONROE WHITE': also sold as 'Monroe #1'; green foliage; white flowers

'SILVERY SUNPROOF': green and white striped foliage; purple flowers

'BIG BLUE' and 'MAJESTIC': green foliage; purple flowers; use in quantity

Ophiopogon japonicus

Not to be confused with Liriope, also known as monkey grass.

Mondo Grass

GETTING ACQUAINTED

Evergreen groundcover

2 to 10 inches high, depending on variety; plants form spreading clumps

Fine, narrow foliage is grasslike and arching; rich, forest green color complements everything

Moderate to rapid rate of growth

Resistant to insects and disease

Tolerates drought

Controls erosion

All-day shade, mostly shady, to half-day's shade; in zones 8 and warmer areas protect from hot afternoon sun in summer

Any well-drained soil

Good choice for planting between stepping stones, brick, or pavers, but not for hot parking areas; use to edge beds, substitute for lawn in small, shady spots, fill empty spaces, and grow in restricted areas or containers; pretty beside garden ponds

Pairs well with aucuba, bluestar, foamflower, Solomon's seal, melampodium, rhododendron, smilax, beautyberry, hosta, Japanese painted fern, wishbone flower, Japanese maple, bleeding heart, Lenten rose, caladium, holly fern, leatherleaf mahonia, dead nettle, redbud, dogwood, Virginia sweetspire, fothergilla, impatiens, celandine poppy, Virginia bluebell, hydrangeas, and pieris

Zones 6–9

The fine-textured, narrow blades of mondo grass contrast well with the large leaves of coarse-textured plants, such as caladium, holly fern, leatherleaf mahonia, and hydrangeas.

Mondo grass is an old standby in Southern shade gardens. Its skinny, arching blades are a delicacy in the landscape, a perfect example of fine-textured foliage. Plants form spreading clumps that eventually blend together like shag carpet. Leaves remain deep green year-round, complementing other plants effortlessly. Of the many attractive companions to mondo grass, hostas stand out. Their large leaves contrast with this groundcover's narrow blades. Colorful plants of all kinds show off nicely against mondo's rich green color.

This groundcover isn't picky about soil as long as its roots can dry out, so avoid planting in wet areas. Mondo grass is quite tolerant of heat and drought, but it grows best when given some shade. Either all-day dappled

shade or half-day's shade is ideal. Some direct sun is fine. The farther south you live, the more important it is to shelter mondo grass from hot afternoon sun during summer. You can also grow this fine groundcover in dark, all-day shade. It will spread more slowly, but plants can live for many years with very little sunlight at all.

Though there are several named selections, *Ophiopogon japonicus* is the plant you'll find most commonly for sale. It is also the one that covers ground the best. Initially, the spread is rather slow, but after the first year mondo grass multiplies more rapidly. This makes mondo grass useful for filling bare spaces in existing beds or for reclaiming areas too shady for lawns to thrive. Plant a lot of mondo grass together to cover ground or tuck a few clumps here and there as filler within beds.

This low groundcover makes an attractive choice for the front layer of beds. However, it will creep into lawns. There's no harm in mowing over unwanted mondo, but you'll notice the dark foliage among the grass. Hard edging set brick-length deep is necessary to keep this groundcover separated

A

B

C

(A) Mondo grass makes an elegant no-mow substitute for lawn in a small, shady area. To get this look, you'll need to weed frequently until the groundcover is thick enough to choke out invaders.
(B) This groundcover's dark green color makes it an attractive filler between other shade-loving plants. Here, mondo grass grows at the foot of foamflower and variegated Solomon's seal.
(C) Mondo grass makes an area rug of dark green that provides the perfect foreground to a shady garden at the Biedenharn Foundation, Monroe, Louisiana

NAMED SELECTIONS

BLACK MONDO GRASS: also sold as *Ophiopogon planiscapus* 'Nigrescens', 'Aribicus', 'Ebony Night', or 'Black Dragon'; shiny black foliage is stunning beside brighter plants; new shoots start off green and quickly turn black; spreads very slowly

'GYOKU RYU': green foliage, just 3 inches high; dense and stiff, not arching; excellent as a living mortar between stepping stones

DWARF MONDO GRASS: also sold as 'Nana' or 'Compactus'; green foliage grows 3 inches high and arches

'BAD HAIR DAY' MONDO GRASS: also sold as *Ophiopogon chingii*; messy green foliage twirls in clumps, 6 inches high by 12 to 15 inches wide; the name alone makes this one irresistible, and it's an attractive plant as well

from lawns. You can plant it where a walkway, drive, or patio will stop its spread; the soft foliage weeping over the paving rim is quite pretty. Shaded, narrow strips of dry soil confined by paving—where few plants will grow—are spots that cry out for mondo grass. You can also grow this groundcover within large beds where it has room to spread unhampered. The more mondo grass you have, the more lush your landscape will look.

MONDO GRASS

Vinca minor

Also sold as littleleaf periwinkle, common periwinkle, creeping myrtle Not to be confused with Madagascar periwinkle (*Vinca rosea* or *Catharanthus roseus*), which is a sun-loving annual with white or hot pink flowers

GETTING ACQUAINTED

Evergreen groundcover

4 to 6 inches high, spreading

Glossy green foliage; lavender flowers in spring

Moderate to rapid rate of growth

Unlikely to thrive in frost-free or rare-frost areas

Partial shade to mostly shady; protect from afternoon sun in summer

Soil that's average to moist and at least somewhat fertile; acidic, neutral, and mildly alkaline soils are fine; not for extremely alkaline or extremely nutrient-deficient soil

Good choice for slopes, large beds, empty spaces beneath deciduous trees, edges of woodlands, beds confined by paving, and dry shade

Pairs well with daffodil, Spanish bluebell, impatiens, wishbone flower, aucuba, dogwood, climbing hydrangea, bluestar, Japanese kerria, hosta, holly fern, rhododendron, aucuba, hydrangeas, star magnolia, Japanese maple, dogwood, pieris, leatherleaf mahonia, Lenten rose, redbud, red buckeye, eastern hemlock, and Solomon's seal

Zones 4–8

Though foliage stays green year-round, littleleaf periwinkle flushes with fresh green growth at bloom time in spring.

Periwinkle

T hink of periwinkle as living mulch. This sprawling groundcover blankets bare spots with a tidy tangle of shiny green leaves. Early spring brings multitudes of flat, bright purple flowers that seem to twinkle among the foliage. Leaves remain green year-round, making periwinkle a landscaping favorite.

There are two kinds of groundcover periwinkle, littleleaf (*Vinca minor*) and bigleaf (*V. major*). Just to make things confusing, the annual *V. rosea* is also called both periwinkle and vinca; it is a heavy bloomer that thrives in full sun and bears white or hot pink flowers. *Vinca rosea* won't spread to

cover ground, and it won't overwinter—so that's not the periwinkle you're looking for to fill empty, shady beds. Look for *V. minor* or *V. major* to get a groundcover.

Both of these groundcover periwinkles thrive in partial shade. All-day dappled shade is fine and so is morning sun followed by afternoon shade. The littleleaf species can also grow in nearly all-day shade, whereas the bigleaf plant needs a little more sun. Both kinds of creeping periwinkle should be protected from hot afternoon summer sun, though *V. minor* will suffer more from leaf scorch than will *V. major*.

Littleleaf periwinkle can take cold winters. It can also take hot, humid summers if planted in adequate shade. Littleleaf periwinkle spreads rapidly in rich, moist soil but it adapts well to less than ideal conditions. Any soil that's fertile to average will do, though plants won't thrive in soil that's exceptionally poor in nutrients. If you've got a shaded bald spot where grass won't grow, littleleaf periwinkle is a solution. This groundcover is also handy for anchoring slopes, filling in beneath shade-loving shrubs, and dressing up natural areas. For a sprawling groundcover, littleleaf periwinkle is quite well behaved. Though it expands its territory with stems that grow, root, and grow some more, this periwinkle is somewhat modest in its quest for new ground. It grows denser with age to make a lovely, leafy carpet. Littleleaf periwinkle won't crawl up trees, shrubs, or walls. It is usually only 3 to 4 inches high and certainly won't get taller

A

B

C

PERIWINKLE

(A) Littleleaf periwinkle easily covers slopes that are shaded by tree canopies in summer.
(B) Littleleaf periwinkle enables you to replace boring brown mulch with a low, spreading carpet of shiny foliage and spring flowers.
(C) It's easy to plant daffodil bulbs beneath a layer of littleleaf periwinkle.

Groundcovers

LITTLELEAF PERIWINKLE, *VINCA MINOR*

'ALBA': green leaves, white flowers

'ATROPURPUREA': green leaves, deep reddish purple flowers

'RALPH SHUGART': green leaves edged with white, bright purple flowers

'TRADITIONAL': green leaves, bright purple flowers

BIGLEAF PERIWINKLE, *VINCA MAJOR*

This groundcover is more aggressive than littleleaf periwinkle. Stems are more likely to run up walls, swarm over small perennials, and sprawl onto paving. Beds of the bigleaf species tend to be filled with mounding foot-high growth as opposed to a flat carpet. But bigleaf periwinkle is very lush. It produces denser greenery than littleleaf periwinkle and larger purple flowers. It is also a little more sun tolerant. However, bigleaf periwinkle is more likely to be damaged by harsh winters than the small-leaved species. Its dislike of cold weather and its ability to thrive in sun make bigleaf periwinkle a better choice for frost-free and rare-frost areas of the South than littleleaf periwinkle.

A variegated cultivar of bigleaf periwinkle (*Vinca major* 'Variegata') is popular for including in container compositions throughout the South. Sea green leaves mottled with cream are very attractive cascading over the sides of pots, planters, raised beds, retaining walls, window boxes, and even hanging baskets. The higher variegated bigleaf periwinkle is elevated, the longer trailers it will produce. When grown in the ground, this variegated selection will sprout upward, tumble over, and grow in a lush, thick tangle.

Bigleaf periwinkle is lush and an enthusiastic grower that can be challenging to contain. It doesn't lie as flat the way the littleleaf species does.

Vinca major 'Variegata' adds a finishing touch to hanging baskets and containers. The cream and green foliage dangles on stringy stems that continue to grow downward.

Variegated bigleaf periwinkle is also useful in planting beds, though it is rather rambunctious once it's let loose in your garden.

The purple flowers of Vinca major *are larger and usually brighter than littleleaf periwinkle blossoms.*

NAMED SELECTIONS—BIGLEAF PERIWINKLE (*VINCA MAJOR*)

'GREEN': green leaves, bright purple flowers

'VARIEGATA': sea green and cream mottled leaves, bright purple flowers

than 6 inches. This plant stays flat—you won't have to trim it and it never produces stray, upright sprouts. The roots of littleleaf periwinkle are thin enough to permit flowering bulbs and other perennials to grow within the same bed. Daffodils do quite well when planted beneath periwinkle. They'll pop through the groundcover in spring to bloom then fade away in summer, leaving periwinkle to provide greenery that camouflages the bulbs' fading foliage.

The best time to start converting bare ground to greenery is in early spring, after the last frost. You can buy periwinkle in pots, but it is a lot less expensive to buy it bare-root if you can find it. Bare-root plants are naked little sprigs that are often sold wrapped in moist newspaper. You'll spend a lot of time on your hands and knees getting all those little plantlets in the ground, but resist the temptation to stuff two or three of them in a hole together; that defeats the purpose. Instead, set each sprig in its own shallow little hole, spacing plants anywhere from 8 to 15 inches apart. Cover exposed soil with mulch to help combat weeds until periwinkle is vigorous enough to choke them out. Water newly planted groundcover immediately. Spring rains should help get the plants growing. Supplement rainfall with sprinklers during hot, dry spells throughout the first growing season. Once established, periwinkle that's not exposed to blazing western sun becomes durable and drought tolerant. It will even grow in those troublesome areas near tree roots, where shade is plentiful but water is not.

You won't have to do anything to maintain littleleaf periwinkle beyond removing any thick layers of fallen leaves that may build up. Decaying leaves are good sources of nutrients for periwinkle, but matted down leaves can prevent photosynthesis from occurring. However, in particularly large beds where leaf removal is impractical, you can just let nature take its course. But keep in mind that, although it is okay to skip raking fallen leaves out of periwinkle, it is never a good idea to rake leaves off the lawn *into* groundcover beds. Piled up leaves will smother periwinkle.

Yellow Archangel

Lamiastrum galeobdolon
'Variegatum'

Also sold as *Lamium galeobdolon,*
Galeobdolon luteum, Lamiastrum
galeobdolon 'Florentinum'

Don't try to grow grass where it doesn't want to grow. All you'll get for your efforts is a bunch of weeds to mow. Instead, hide your shame by covering bare ground with a plant intended to do just that—a groundcover. Yellow archangel is an attractive, fast-growing groundcover that's ideal for large shady areas where grass refuses to cooperate.

Sprig a shaded, barren bed with baby yellow archangels, and eventually it will be filled with a thick cover of heavenly foliage. Each 2-inch oval leaf is green marked generously with silver. Though the clusters of lemony flowers that appear in spring are pretty, you'll love this plant for the way its attractive foliage fills empty areas. Sprawling stems root themselves where they touch soil, forming new plants that continue sprawling and rooting. This habit of growth makes yellow archangel a good choice for anchoring slopes. Give this plant plenty of room to spread.

Moist, fertile soil will prompt lush growth that covers ground the quickest, but you can grow yellow archangel in dry soil, too. Though it spreads more slowly where water and sunlight are scarce, this enthusiastic plant will tackle the difficult zone dominated by tree roots. I've even planted it beneath eastern hemlocks that unfortunately had their lowest limbs removed before they were mine. I don't water these location-challenged archangels, fertilize them, or even mulch them; fallen hemlock needles and blown-in oak leaves take care of that. The groundcover just creeps along there growing slowly, but it produces rich foliage nonetheless. Elsewhere in my garden, yellow archangel easily fills a big slope beneath a large burr oak. Given a bit more sunlight and

GETTING ACQUAINTED

Evergreen groundcover

8 to 12 inches high, spreads far and wide

Rambling, spreading stems bear bright green leaves decorated with silver stripes; yellow flowers in spring

Rapid rate of growth

Partial shade to mostly shady; protect from afternoon sun in summer

Any soil except wet

Good choice for growing in shady, damp areas or in dry shade beneath large trees; grow in natural areas, on slopes, and in front of decks so it will creep under them; not for perennial beds or small, confined areas; will sprawl over paving

Pairs well with rhododendron, pieris, Japanese kerria, Japanese maple, eastern hemlock, red buckeye, redbud, star magnolia, blue-star, dogwood, beautyberry, Pinxterbloom azalea, fothergilla, Virginia sweetspire, gooseneck loosestrife, leatherleaf mahonia, and oakleaf hydrangea

Zones 4–9

Yellow archangel is adaptable and aggressive. It will even grow beneath maple trees. You can tuck pockets of soil around shallow tree roots to give the groundcover enough ground to get started.

Groundcovers

(A) Talk about tough—this groundcover will even work its way up through a thick layer of fallen oak leaves year after year. So don't worry about getting fallen leaves out of yellow archangel beds, but don't rake leaves into them, either.

(B) Yellow archangel stays somewhat green year-round, but it flushes with a fresh crop of striped foliage each spring.

(C) Yellow flowers appear on new stems in spring.

A

B

C

COVERING GROUND

Buying large groundcover plants means you get started with more roots but you'll spend more money. If plants cost more, you're likely to buy too few of them and spread them too far apart to get good coverage. Instead, purchase quantities of small plants and plan to spend a lot of time on your hands and knees. Space little yellow archangels from 8 to 15 inches apart. You might have to water a little if the weather's hot, but once new plants show signs of putting out fresh leaves, you can pretty much forget about them. At planting, mulch the bed to discourage weed growth while the young plants get settled. Eventually, yellow archangel will produce a thick mat of foliage that will smother weeds—you won't need to continue to apply mulch. Yellow archangel will also choke perennials, so don't include this plant in perennials beds. To speed growth in beds where topsoil has washed away, layer rotting leaves over the bed and plant yellow archangel through it. Squirt the young groundcover with a hose whenever you happen to have one handy.

rainfall, these plants were sufficiently motivated to completely carpet the area with a tangle of leafy stems in a mere two years. If you're willing to set up sprinklers, you can coax even faster coverage from your yellow archangels.

Partial shade is the best condition for growing this groundcover. All-day dappled shade or morning sun followed by afternoon shade are both agreeable to yellow archangel. Dark, all-day shade is not—the silvery stripes fade away without a little sunlight to encourage the foliage variegation. Growth rates are severely compromised in all-day shade, too. But, if you've got such a spot and nothing else is working, go ahead and give yellow archangel a try. Though the leaves may be plain green and stems may spread slowly, that's probably better than bare ground.

Sometimes stopping a plant is more challenging than getting it going. Yellow archangel that's content in its setting can be such a plant. It has an indefinite spread, so this sprawling groundcover is only going to cease conquering new ground when it meets with a lawnmower or reaches the limits of partial shade. This plant is in the mint family—if you've ever grown mint, you know how quickly it fills in. Make sure you're prepared for such botanical bounty before you set yellow archangel loose in your landscape.

Vines

Climbing Hydrangea

Hydrangea anomala petiolaris

Also sold as *Hydrangea petiolaris*

GETTING ACQUAINTED

Deciduous vine (bare in winter)

30 to 50 feet high by 6 to 8 feet wide

Bushy branches of heart-shaped leaves; large, cream-colored lacy blooms borne in early to late spring cover mature plants

Slow rate of growth for first two to five years; rapid growth after that

Partial shade, requires some sun to bloom; in zone 8 protect from afternoon sun in summer

Moist, fertile soil is best; will adapt to dry soil

Good choice for outbuildings, tall chimneys, blank walls, and growing on thick tree trunks with high branches; attractive when swarming over stumps, low walls, and split rail fences; not for growing on wooden houses, because it must be cut down to paint or stain siding and aerial rootlets may damage wood

Pairs well with Japanese kerria, melampodium, aucuba, periwinkle, and large hardwood trees

Zones 4 to 8

Autumn leaves are attractive, though not spectacular, on most climbing hydrangeas grown in the South. The vines are bare in winter.

W hen I first met a climbing hydrangea years ago, I couldn't hide my surprise. Who knew? It was like suddenly discovering that cats secretly love to swim.

Climbing hydrangeas require patience, fertile soil, and shade—and these are listed in order of importance. Patience is essential as this plant will do nothing but sit there for years after you plant it. All of its initial energy goes into establishing a strong root system. That's all well and good for the vine, but pretty boring for the gardener. It helps to know that you've done nothing wrong. Your climbing hydrangea hasn't rejected you and there's no need to develop some drastic fertilizing or pruning program. Just leave the plant alone and find some weeds to pull.

After a good three or even five years of very little in the way of interesting development, your climbing hydrangea will surprise you with a sudden interest in living up to now-faded expectations. With a good foundation underground, this vine can concentrate on growing up and out. Up can mean reaching an eventual vertical destination some 50 feet or more above the ground, if the supporting structure is that tall. Out can mean a bushy roundness of 6 feet. Indeed, a mature climbing hydrangea looks like a shrub gone haywire, but in a beautiful sort of way. Whatever you do, don't cut the bushiness off. The lateral branches that grow away from the wall are the ones that bear the blossoms. After waiting for years, it would be criminal to deprive yourself of flowers in the name of tidying up.

Climbing hydrangea attaches itself to supporting structures by means of hairy little aerial rootlets. These clever devices suction right onto surfaces, smooth or rough, so there's no need to give this vine a post or

A

B

C

D

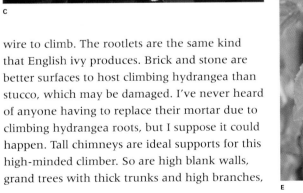

E

wire to climb. The rootlets are the same kind that English ivy produces. Brick and stone are better surfaces to host climbing hydrangea than stucco, which may be damaged. I've never heard of anyone having to replace their mortar due to climbing hydrangea roots, but I suppose it could happen. Tall chimneys are ideal supports for this high-minded climber. So are high blank walls, grand trees with thick trunks and high branches,

(A) Now is not the time to be thrifty. Because climbing hydrangea concentrates on growing roots for years before it puts on height, it is a good idea to by the largest one you can find. *Photo courtesy of Leslie J. Turek*

(B) Even when blossoms age and petals are few, climbing hydrangea retains an appealingly layered look.

(C) Lacy flowers every spring are the reward for patient gardeners who wait years for their climbing hydrangea to show an interest in both climbing and blooming. *Photo courtesy of Leslie J. Turek*

(D) The jagged-edged leaves of climbing hydrangea are nearly heart-shaped.

(E) Climbing hydrangea clings to surfaces by producing aerial rootlets along its stems. It can grow straight up a flat wall.

Vines

old stumps, the sides of outbuildings, and even low walls that vines can swarm over.

Do be aware that if you pull a climbing hydrangea down, it will leave footprints behind. You should also know that climbing hydrangea is deciduous. The shiny green leaves turn yellow in autumn before dropping. I find the bare, cinnamon-colored stems attractive, but if the thought of a leafless vine plastered to a wall in winter bothers you, don't plant climbing hydrangea.

But here's what you'll be missing. This vine is the living definition of picturesque when it blooms. The flowers are 4 to 6 inches across. Creamy outer petals—fertile flowers themselves, actually—surround an inner doily of tiny sterile flowers. These showy blossoms appear after climbing hydrangea is fully leafed out, so you get the full impact of cream against green. Climbing hydrangeas need shade in our hot climate, but make sure vines get a little sun to promote flowering. Morning sun or dappled sun filtered through tree canopies will do.

Smilax

Smilax smallii

Also sold as Jackson vine, bamboo vine, lanceleaf greenbrier, *Smilax lanceolata*

Blame it on kudzu, Japanese honeysuckle, or any number of climbing, twisting, smothering invaders. We Southerners are much too hesitant to plant vines in our gardens. But homeowners in historic Huntsville, Alabama, are cultivating an old tradition. They're fearlessly festooning their porches with a thornless evergreen vine that they call Jackson vine and horticulturists call smilax. The effect is charming without being cute, elegant without being clipped. In today's transient society, a vine-trimmed porch lends an air of permanence. That's not just a house beneath that vine; it's an established home.

Smilax is a wiry thing and its puny flowers aren't worth noticing. Only female plants produce berries, and although the blue-black drooping clusters are nice, they're not spectacular. So what's the appeal of smilax? The foliage. The leaves are green on both sides and they stay that way all year. Smilax doesn't have an off-season. The topsides of leaves are glossy, adding subtle sparkle to the shadows.

Smilax smallii is a well-behaved cousin of that pesky wild vine, greenbrier (*S. bona-nox*). The latter has killer thorns, incredibly heavy tuberous roots, and seems to stretch for many tangled miles. The *S. smallii* species that you buy in nurseries has no thorns and grows more sedately. It is easily house-trained and will grow neatly where you want it to go. The stems produce tendrils that twine around supports; this vine won't damage wood or brick. The clever Huntsvillians who employ smilax so tastefully train it on chains held in place by hooks. The vine weaves its way through the chain, concealing it, while decorating the eaves of a porch, railing, or archway over a door. When it is time to paint the house, the homeowner simply unhooks the vine-encrusted

GETTING ACQUAINTED

Evergreen vine

20 to 30 feet long, sprawling

Thornless vine with year-round shiny green foliage

Slow to moderate rate of growth

Tolerates drought

Resistant to insects and disease

Partial shade to all-day shade; tolerates morning sun

Any soil, wet or dry

Good choice for training along eaves of porches, rails, archways, fences, and arbors; suitable for beach houses; will not damage wooden structures

Pairs well with hosta, liriope, mondo grass, Virginia sweetspire, bluestar, fothergilla, Pinxterbloom azalea, dead nettle, Japanese kerria, aucuba, camellia, rhododendron, and Solomon's seal

Zones 7–10

Smilax is a gentle evergreen vine that adds storybook charm to any house.

Most of the lush foliage occurs on the overhead portion of the vine with the lower stems serving merely to plug the plant into the ground.

chain and lays the whole thing gently on the ground until the final coat is dry. Then, the vine goes back up.

Another lovely feature of smilax is its adaptability. This vine won't get thin if it lacks sunlight. You can grow it in all-day shade or partial shade. Dappled shade is good, and so is a half-day's shade (it doesn't matter which half). Smilax isn't picky about soil, either. It will grow equally well in wet or dry soil. You may have to shop carefully to locate smilax for sale, but it is a good vine to find. And the sooner, the better—smilax can be slow to get started. But don't despair. Once your vine has finally decided to accept the position you've offered it, the pace of growth will improve. It may take several years before smilax drapes like a living garland from one end of a porch to the other, but then the branching sprays of foliage thicken effortlessly.

Page numbers in **boldface** are main entries.

Index